The Joy of Color

Fair Isle Knitting Your Way

Janine Bajus
the feral knitter

Published in 2016 by Willa Jane Press.

Second printing 2017

Text copyright © 2016 by Janine Bajus.

ISBN 978-0-9975234-0-9

Please contact the author for permission to teach from this book and for class handouts.

Book Design: Kate Godfrey | okaykate

Photographs copyright © 2016 by Janine Bajus unless otherwise noted below.
Stitch Definition: Cover & pages 1, 3, 5, 7-9, 24-25, 36, 60-61, 80-81, 88, 100-101, 105, 122-123, 137, 140.
Kevin Candland Photography: Yarn photos on pages 4, 11, 15, 17, 26, 30, 31, 45, 47, 50, 53, 75, 77, 79, 97, 99, 119, 121, 131, 134.
Student pages: Courtesy of the designers.
Carolyn Foss: 47 (middle).
fibre space, Alexandria, VA: 38 (wall of yarn).
Meg Swansen: 62 (inspiration).
Rebecca Redston: 102.
Karen Hust: 109 (cats).

Printed and bound in China

Willa Jane Press
1153 the Alameda
Berkeley CA 94707

This book is dedicated to every knitter who has said, "I wish I could do that."

Contents

And suddenly you just know:
It is time to start something new
and trust the magic of beginnings.

— MEISTER ECKHART

FOREWORD

The Joy of Color, indeed! It is difficult to imagine a time when Janine Bajus was not a two-color knitter. But she is a truthful woman, and swears that when we met at Knitting Camp in 1998, she had never knitted a Fair Isle garment.

Many knitters possess the manual skill to produce a Fair Isle sweater and can follow an existing design with no difficulty. They may even have the ability to design original motifs, place them, and calculate a perfect fit from their gauge. But... choosing the shades for a multiple-color garment is an art unto itself. With over 200 Shetland wool shades from which to choose, you can pull out skeins of all the colors you see in your favorite painting, and they look wonderful lying side by side on the sofa. However, when knitted—one intermingled with another—the colors shift before your eyes, often resulting in a muddy or blurred effect, rendering the motif nearly invisible.

Janine is a master of color, and swatching is the key. Over many years of knitting Fair Isle garments, Janine has developed a unique and superior set of instructions which simplify the daunting task of—not only selecting, but placing the different colors. Patience is required, but is rewarded by the assurance that you can cast on a full 300+ stitch sweater body and know that your color choices will work. And, as a species, are not Knitters a patient lot? One stitch at a time...

Not only does the author generously share all the tricks that heretofore were available only to her students, but we get to see thirteen splendid examples of finished garments, all designed and knitted from scratch by her skillful pupils.

Through this lovely book, we all can take Janine's class and become our own designers of multiple-colored garments.

Meg Swansen
Schoolhouse Press

> JANINE IS A MASTER OF COLOR, AND SWATCHING IS THE KEY. OVER MANY YEARS OF KNITTING FAIR ISLE GARMENTS, JANINE HAS DEVELOPED A UNIQUE AND SUPERIOR SET OF INSTRUCTIONS WHICH SIMPLIFY THE DAUNTING TASK OF—NOT ONLY SELECTING, BUT PLACING THE DIFFERENT COLORS.

WELCOME, KNITTER!

1976: *Spinning wool while wearing my grandmother's gift of a Fair Isle yoke sweater.*

2013: *At the Taos Wool Festival in Taos, New Mexico.*

My grandmother bought me a Fair Isle yoke sweater in the 1960s—I remember the joy of picking through a pile of colors, eventually settling on one with a moorit body. That sweater followed me through college.

When I learned to knit 30 years later I hungered to use color, lots of color, in the Fair Isle tradition but I didn't know where to start.

In 1998, having been a knitter for two years, I attended Meg Swansen's Knitting Camp in Marshfield, Wisconsin—the creative energy in the room blew me away. Meg made an announcement: they were having a Fair Isle contest! As she laid out the rules, memories of my well-loved yoke sweater flooded me and I thought to myself: "I wish I were a good enough knitter to knit a Fair Isle."

At next year's Camp the entries came pouring in, a welter of color and pattern that made us all gasp in wonder. Once again I felt that longing to design and knit such beautiful garments. Deep in my heart, though, I believed that you needed something special, something inborn, coupled with decades of knitting experience, to be able to do this, whereas I was a fairly new knitter with no art school background.

But something extraordinary happened: One of the designers decided to fix a flaw in her garment during Camp, and I watched her re-knit the hem. She worked slowly, forming each stitch one after the other—and I suddenly realized that I could do THAT!

Energized, I went home and immediately cast on for a stranded design in Shetland jumperweight wool. I watched Meg Swansen's Fair Isle Vest video over and over again as I persevered, learning garment construction techniques as I honed my two-color knitting skills.

And then the desire to make my own visions manifest took over, and my creative life as Feral Knitter began.

I began to explore the history of Fair Isle knitting, how its use of color differs from that of other stranded knitting traditions, how I could create my own motifs, how stranded garments could be shaped—well, there is no end to the possibilities!

When others asked me to teach them how to design their own sweaters, I relied on my training as a technical writer to break down my process into repeatable steps. Hundreds of knitters have taken my 3-day Design Your Own Fair Isle workshop. What you hold in your hands is that workshop, expanded, in written form.

Where will *The Joy of Color* take you?

In *The Joy of Color* I will walk you through a tried-and-true process that can be followed step by step: First, you will define the your project; second, you will choose your colors; then the motifs; and finally the garment shape.

Each chapter includes a **Workshop section** to guide you, as well as a list of my favorite resources on the subject for further exploration and some words of wisdom to inspire you.

Sprinkled throughout you will find **Gallery pages** that highlight the experience of some of my students—they bravely share the ideas that changed as they went along, the swatches that didn't work, the decisions they made, their hard-won advice, and their lovely sweaters.

In **Case Studies** you will see how some of my designs developed, from initial concept to finished garment. To round out the book I've included chapters on **techniques** specific to stranded knitting and, perhaps most important of all, on **getting it done**.

Words of encouragement

If I could stand beside you as you design your sweater, this is what you would hear me say:

- Don't intellectualize—play with the yarn.
- Simplify, simplify, simplify.
- There is potential in every swatch.
- You can do it!

I hope you spend many happy hours turning your dream into reality, enjoying a sense of competence and relishing your creative freedom. Now, get started!

Janine, the Feral Knitter
Berkeley, California, 2016

Why "Feral Knitter"?

When I was first learning Fair Isle design I wanted to find people who were similarly obsessed with color and pattern. I put an ad into my knitting guild's newsletter; someone called while a non-knitting friend was visiting.

When I finished the phone call, my friend said, in a voice tinged with worry, "Janine, WHAT is a feral knitter?"

And that misunderstanding stuck!

Feral knitting is the recognition that there is no one right answer—there are millions of choices, the process is messy and non-linear, and despite color wheels and color theories and books galore, the only judge of "rightness" is the knitter's own delight.

Getting Started

* What is Fair Isle knitting?

* Creating your own design

* Feral rules

* The yarn

CREATING YOUR OWN DESIGN

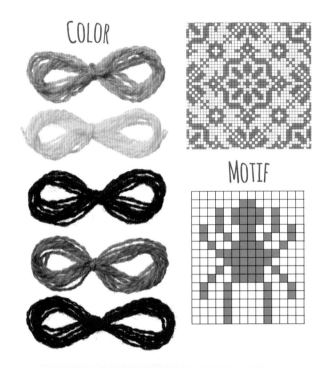

COLOR

MOTIF

From initial concept, to color, to motif, to garment shape—breaking down the process into manageable steps leads to a garment you will love.

GARMENT SHAPE

Designing a Fair Isle garment from scratch can seem daunting because each major element that combines to make the final design—the color, the motif, and the garment shape—is influenced by the others.

When things get complex remind yourself that most projects can be approached piece by piece. By working on these main components of Fair Isle design—color, motif, and garment shape—one at a time what seems impossibly convoluted suddenly opens up.

Here are the four basic steps:

- Define the project.

- Choose your colors.

- Find motifs and add your colors.

- Work out the garment shape, motif placement, and construction details.

Along the way you will, no doubt, have to revisit some decisions—the process is far from linear—but you won't feel stuck in quicksand.

Follow me into an exciting exploration of color, pattern, and three-dimensional shapes that just might take over your life!

WHAT IS FAIR ISLE KNITTING?

But before we go any further, let's try to define our terms. Fair Isle knitting is a distinctive type of stranded color knitting that developed roughly 150 years ago on Fair Isle, part of the Shetland Island archipelago north of Scotland.

Lace and hosiery knitted goods were already important Shetland exports when the multicolored patterned knitting entered the picture; references to colorful knitting began to appear in the early 19th century. Stranded knitting was a common technique throughout Europe, and Shetland was at the center of a lively trade with Holland, Germany, the Baltic states, the British Isles, and Scandinavia—their influences are clear in the earliest knitted samples, which date from the 1850s. Patterned sweaters, stockings, gloves, and hats were knit for export, which affected the evolution of the patterns.

From Decade to Decade

Pinning down "traditional Fair Isle" is more complex that it might appear at first. Sarah Laurensen said it best in *Shetland Textiles: 800 BC to the Present*:

> There is no moment in history, nor is there a garment, which can be held up as the definitive example of what Fair Isle actually is. Since its beginnings the craft has been varied and fluid, a revolving door of influences with no geographical boundaries. As a technique Fair Isle knitting follows certain principles, but allows for infinite variation.... It is the ever-shifting nature of Fair Isle that characterises the craft, making it endlessly creative and expressive while ensuring it remains utterly distinctive in all its forms.

Any discussion of traditional Fair Isle knitting needs to take into account the significant changes in Fair Isle knitting over the decades; what was the tradition in 1850 was not the tradition in 1895 or 1928 or 1960. Fair Isle motifs, edge treatments, and color choices changed in response to new production methods, economic competition, and the dictates of fashion.

For example, the earliest Fair Isle colorwork pieces were knit in natural sheep's color wool that might be naturally dyed in shades of blue, red, or yellow. Motifs were not necessarily aligned vertically and color changes did not always happen in logical relation to the motifs. Very quickly, however, vertical alignment and matching color changes to motifs became standard.

When synthetic dyes became widely available in the late 1800s, Fair Isle knitters began to make very bright color choices. In the 1930s this candy-box look was superseded by sweaters knit with all natural shades of Shetland as the industry responded to competition and attempted to brand itself.

Changes to the tradition continued: Motifs from Norway were incorporated into Fair Isle visual vocabulary in the 1940s, knitting machines came into wide use in the 1950s, and the Fair Isle yoke sweater was ubiquitous in the 1960s and today.

So how do we answer the question, "What is Fair Isle knitting?" I've examined the stranded knitting traditions of many cultures to arrive at a working definition.

BEAUTY FROM NECESSITY

The fact that Fair Isle knitting was primarily an economic function influenced the development of what we now consider traditional colors, patterning, and construction. Above all, the knitting had to be efficient.

* The patterns and color movement are usually **symmetrical**—they move into a center point and then mirror that movement out again. This makes it easier to knit without relying on charts.

* Motifs are **centered** above each other.

* A "**pop**" color is often placed at the center point of the motif.

* **Only two colors are** used per round.

* The pattern color and the background color usually don't change in the same row within a motif.

* There are **no abrupt changes** in value

* Floats are shorter than 1 inch.

* No purl or slipped stitches are used.

* The garment is knit **in the round**, to save time in finishing and free the knitter from counting to match pieces.

* **Steeks** are used to make it possible to knit the entire garment in the round.

Despite the drudgery of market knitting many knitters made special garments for themselves or their families, taking greater liberties with patterning, shaping, and motifs, just as we modern knitters do.

THE DRAGONFLY RIVER VEST

FOR MY FIRST PROJECT I wanted to design a vest based on my favorite backpacking and fishing destination: Bridge Creek, in the North Cascades.

My first swatch shows that I was set on using figurative motifs: trees, tents, stars, water, and rainbow trout. My color choices were very symbolic—even though the actual creek is a steely translucent gray with a rusty undertone, I was stuck on "water equals blue." I'd heard that Fair Isle designs require pop colors. What could be more of a pop than the bright orange (reflecting the sunset)? Although I had a vague understanding of value gradients, I didn't understand value contrast.

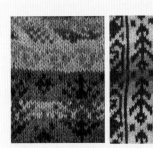

My first swatch (left) versus my final design (right). Two different ways to approach trees and water.

RE-STARTING The entire swatch was knit at 6 stitches per inch because I had not yet figured out how to couple tight stitches with loose floats. Altogether, a well-meaning disaster.

Nothing to be done but throw it all out and start over. My next vision, a pullover, seemed too complex, so I measured my favorite fleece vest and started yet again, more simply! A solid dark blue pattern against a gradated background seemed more doable. The colors were straightforward: shades of blues and greens, five rounds of each. While exploring colors for this vest I developed the speed swatch for color (page 39) to hurry the process along.

I sketched out simplified tree and dragonfly patterns on graph paper. The swirly pattern is modified from the Deli Kivrim chart in Betsy Harrell's *Charted Anatolian Designs*—it reminded me of whirlpools. None of the three motifs has the same row count, but I wasn't worried about it. I photocopied the motifs and taped together various combinations until I hit on one I liked.

The same inspiration, very different results. ❖

My second sketch, again too complex. I simplified my motifs when I simplified my color choices.

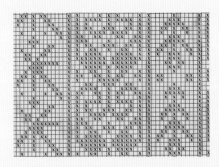

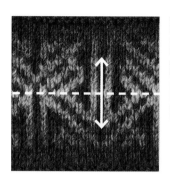

Fair Isle colorwork depends on the controlled sequencing of colors by value, mirroring, and value contrast working together to create its lovely light-on-water effect.

Feral Fair Isle

What separates Fair Isle colorwork from other types of stranded colorwork is the controlled sequencing of colors by value (darkness or lightness) coupled with the mirroring of pattern and value sequences in tandem. Sequencing plus mirroring creates the luminous, three-dimensional effect that sets Fair Isle design apart.

Sounds complex, but don't worry—I'll cover these concepts more fully in the next chapter.

Let's Begin!

When you start designing your Fair Isle garment you have an infinity of choices. Time spent at the start defining the project will be repaid a thousandfold by giving you confidence in all your decisions as you walk through the design process. Before you grab the yarn and pick up your needles, answer five basic questions about your project:

Who? **Who is this garment for?**

You probably have a vague idea of the garment you want to make. Think about it as part of your life. Is this something you will wear, really? Are the colors flattering? Is the design flattering? Are the motifs suitable to your personality? Is this garment useful within your larger wardrobe (we often forget about this, don't we)? It is particularly important to ask these questions if you are designing a sweater for someone else.

Feral Rules for Modern Fair Isle

Modern knitters, freed from the demands of production knitting and the strictures of tradition—and with access to more colors and yarns than ever before—can make their design decisions based on personal preference. Whether you choose to work within more traditional Fair Isle structures or plan to make a garment that's entirely original, there are three hard and fast rules.

Feral Rule #1: *Do what you want.* You will hear many opinions about the right way to combine colors and patterns, but these are just opinions, they are not objective facts. You will have to rely on your own sense of what works.

Feral Rule #2: *There is no one right way to do it.* This rule might seem inconsequential, but more often than not the thing holding us back is a sense that there is an objective standard that we are failing to meet. When you are getting the results you want at each stage of the design process you can move ahead. Don't overwork your idea!

Feral Rule #3: *There is no way to determine with certainty what will look good without swatching.* In Fair Isle knitting, the colors are interacting on a small scale, which creates what is known as optical blending. How the colors work together changes when their proportions change, or when one color is substituted for another. Color pencils and color charting programs simply cannot be trusted to capture the effect of the yarns as they interact. Luckily, swatching for color can be pretty exciting!

What If I've NEVER Knit Fair Isle BEFORE?

Fair Isle designs look trickier to knit than they really are. To be successful you simply need to get comfortable handling two yarns at the same time.

If you've never tried knitting with two colors, check out DVDs, online classes, and videos (see Techniques for more information about holdng the yarns). You will feel awkward at first—learning any new fine motor skill takes time.

Hats and cowls—any items that can be knit on a 16" or longer circular needle—are excellent first projects.

One student showed up in class who could not remember how to cast on, but she went on to design marvelous tams and sweaters! You will be successful if you are curious, willing to make mistakes and keep going.

WHAT? What kind of a garment are you thinking of?

Would your sporty sister really wear something with blousy sleeves? Would your daughter living in Berkeley really need a stranded sweater knit in worsted-weight yarn?

WHEN? When can you envision wearing this?

Will this shawl be worn to an opera opening in San Francisco or tossed over a t-shirt for walking the dog? If you envision a pullover to be worn while raking leaves, jewel tones of the Caribbean might not be the note you want to strike. And if you are thinking of a workaday garment, should the sweater have kimono sleeves that cover the hands?

WHERE? Where will the garment be worn?

If you are knitting a garment to protect against extreme air-conditioning in Phoenix it will probably differ from a sweater knit for Minneapolis winters. A sophisticated jacket for a dinner out will look different than one planned for the ski slope.

WHY? A personalized Fair Isle garment deserves respect.

Respect yourself by knitting only for those you love who under-stand the time and artistry involved.

We knitters have been guilty, from time to time, of knitting out of a mixture of ego, enthusiasm, desire to try something new, and good intentions; sadly, the result of these motives is often that the garment lies unworn and unloved in the back of a closet. This process of questioning is designed to keep this from happening so you end up with a garment that will be loved for decades.

Don't worry if you don't have answers to all of these questions when you start out, but it is important that you keep the questions in mind as you work on your design. When you find yourself stuck, taking a look at your notes can help clarify your path.

The Yarn

Fair Isle colorwork was traditionally knit with 2-ply yarns spun from the soft fleece of Shetland sheep. These sheep sport a very wide range of natural colors, ranging from deep brown ("Shetland black"), to reddish brown ("moorit"), to fawn, to natural white, and shades of gray. These natural wools were often overdyed with indigo (blue), madder (red), and local plants (yellow). Jamieson & Smith Wool Brokers has partnered with the Shetland Textile Museum to replicate the original semi-worsted grist and colors of the earliest examples of Fair Isle colorwork in their Shetland Heritage line.

Different types of yarn

Modern 2-ply jumperweight yarn (jumper is British for "pullover") is spun a little more woolen than the original; that is, it is a little loftier and has a more pronounced halo.

Classic Shetland jumperweight wool
Woolen spun, 2-ply, with a fair amount of grabbiness or stickiness and a lovely halo that helps blend colors. Approximately 110-120 yards per oz (~105 m/25 g), knit at 7-9 stitches per inch. Some yarns in this category: *Jamieson's Shetland Spindrift, Jamieson & Smith 2-ply Jumperweight, Elemental Affects Natural Shetland Fingering, Harrisville Shetland, Blackberry Ridge Fingering Weight.*

Slightly softer and squishier yarns
Woolen spun, 2-ply, ~115 yards per oz. Some yarns in this category: *Brown Sheep Fingering, Cascade Fingering, KnitPicks Palette, Brooklyn Tweed Loft.*

Virtual Yarns Hebridean 2-ply
Woolen, 2-ply, ~ 88 m/25 g, slightly thicker than regular jumperweight.

Scandinavian yarns
These hard-wearing yarns are worsted spun, with a distinct sheen and no haloing. Some yarns in this category: *Rauma Finullgarn, Dale Garn Daletta.*

From Natural Colors to Bright

Shetland Black

Gray

Moorit

Indigo

Fawn

Madder

Natural White

Yellow

When synthetic dyes were made widely available in the late 1800s, Fair Isle knitters added brighter colors to the traditional palette. Modern knitters can choose from hundreds of colors.

Acorn Sweater

Nontraditional pairings can lead to wonderful designs: curry spice colors applied to a Celtic motif. I tested several pop colors to find one that worked.

I WANTED TO KNIT a sweater for my husband, John. By identifying who the sweater was for I'd already resolved a number of design decisions: no pink, nothing flashy, simple shape. I began by asking him what kind of sweater he would like: Sleeves or vest? Pullover or cardigan? V-neck or crew neck?

Then I asked him to tell me what color he would like. He said he'd like a brown sweater. I found a photo of curry spices in a spice catalog that he approved.

John does not like to wear flashy clothing, so I knew that I would need to find an indistinct, small, repeating motif. No big patterns and no whimsical stuff! His under-stated style also dictated that I would need to use a fairly close set of values in my sequences to avoid a strongly horizontal look.

COLOR & PATTERN I found a Celtic key motif in Co Spinhoven's *Celtic Charted Designs* that fit the bill, but I also wanted to put a personal stamp on the sweater. On the sides I added a narrow pattern of acorns because John has a habit of picking them up while we are on walks. This acorn motif is small and doesn't draw attention to itself.

I decided to make Shetland Black, a deep natural brown, the dominant color by using it for the pattern; the four colors of the background move from a medium-light value to a medium dark value. This was such a simple color story that I didn't do a speed swatch for color.

Choosing a pop color proved to be problematic. I had originally placed a mustard yellow at the turn point, but when I viewed the motif swatch it was obvious that this color was too discreet. I went back to my inspiration and noticed that I hadn't used the green of the bay leaves in the photo. After duplicate stitching three different greens onto the swatch I decided on one that seemed way too bright in the ball but was toned down and just right in the pattern.

The sweater itself is a simple inset drop-sleeve design with shaped shoulders; the sleeves are knit from the shoulder down with some added interest in the faux broken corrugated rib. ❖

The handsome model wearing the sweater is not my husband, but he looks great in it, too. Little touches will make your design one-of-a-kind. I added John's name in the side motif and chose a broken corrugated rib.

Many other yarn companies produce yarns that can be used for stranded knitting—I have concentrated on 2-ply fingering weight wools that come in a wide range of colors, but feel free to explore others: cashmere-merino blends, for example, Icelandic unspun singles, or lace weight yarns. New yarns for stranded designs are appearing every day—this is a good time to be a knitter!

You can create stranded garments out of slicker or heavier yarns, such as cotton, alpaca, silk, or superwash merino. It is more difficult to handle slick yarns when stranding, and steeking these types of yarns requires special care, but there are situations when non-wool or machine washable yarns are needed. Fair Isle sweaters made in worsted weight yarns can be very heavy but useful for outerwear.

Combining Yarn Types

You can mix and match yarn lines within the same garment— you can successfully mix Jamieson's Shetland Spindrift, Jamieson & Smith 2-ply Jumperweight, and Elemental Affects Natural Shetland Fingering yarns within a sweater, for example. Swatch to make sure that differences in yarn structure and weight don't disrupt your design.

What to Look For

You want to choose a yarn line that has a wide range of colors, that does not regularly retire colors, and that you enjoy knitting with. Don't stint on quality. Although a Fair Isle sweater in high-quality yarn might cost more, your cost per hour of knitting enjoyment is actually very low. You are creating a unique garment that will take hours of your time; don't compromise when purchasing yarn for the project.

SOME YARN SAMPLES

Classic Shetland Jumperweight Wool
Jamieson's Shetland Spindrift

Historic Shetland
Jamieson & Smith Heritage

Single Ply
Istex Plötulopi Unspun Icelandic

American Shetland
Elemental Affects Natural Shetland Fingering

Mixed fibers
Plucky Oxford Merino & cashmere

All shown at 70%.

Building A Yarn Library

Designing your own garments is much easier if you can look at your color options in person rather than online. Very few yarn shops can afford to carry all the colors of any given yarn line—if you live near one of them please support it by purchasing your yarn there.

Most people will have to shop for yarns online; given the difficulties of capturing colors correctly on a computer monitor this can be frustrating, costly, and time consuming, so you will probably want to build your own yarn collection.

Start by ordering the color card for the yarn line you want to use and then begin to build your library:

Build your yarn library organically over time. Start with any leftovers in your stash. Then purchase colors for your first design, which adds more leftovers to the stash. After that, buy five or six balls every month, concentrating on your favorite color families but trying to add colors that aren't in your comfort zone as well. Eventually you will have built a useful yarn library while staying within a budget.

Go in with a few friends to purchase an entire set of colors. Divide each ball by the number of participants. These miniskeins might not be enough for your all your swatching needs, but at least you will be able to accurately judge which colors to order for your project.

Purchase a single ball of each available color. This can be an expensive proposition, but many retailers offer a discount when you order a full line.

To Do

1 Create a mini journal or start a page in your knitting journal. The Toolkit at right is full of content suggestions.

2 Date those entries! (Really, do this!) Your design is part of a story, and it's fun and instructive to keep good records of your process.

3 Write down your answers to the five basic questions: *Who*, *What*, *When*, *Where*, and *Why*. Your answers can be lengthy or short, so long as you give them some thought and make a record of your intentions.

   These answers will guide the rest of your design decisions—you can return to them if you get stuck. And taking time at the beginning to articulate your intentions can help you avoid many mistakes.

To Explore

Alice Starmore's Book of Fair Isle Knitting by Alice Starmore. *An excellent, comprehensive history, pattern, and technical resource for Fair Isle knitting.*

A Shetland Knitter's Notebook by Mary Smith and Chris Bunyan. *History, economics, and personalities of the Shetland knitting traditions.*

Shetland Textiles: 800 BC to the Present Edited by Sarah Laurensen. *A gorgeous look at the landscape of Shetland and its textile history.*

To Inspire

When I consider a new project, I begin with obvious concerns: fiber, pattern, color, and tactile qualities. A sometimes unspoken—perhaps less conscious thought comes from my emotional experience of the person to whom I will present the finished article (including myself). My bond with the receiver, my awareness of that person's spirit, patience, and flexibility—all come into play. **— ROBIN GRACE**

There is a vitality, a life force, an energy, a quickening that is translated through you into action; and because there is only one of you in all time, this expression is unique. If you block it, it will never exist through any other medium and it will be lost. The world will not have it. You must keep that channel open. It is not for you to determine how good it is, nor how valuable. **— MARTHA GRAHAM**

DREAMING & PLANNING & REVISING

It is very important that you find a way to collect and store your planning notes that works for you.

I found that a large journal did not work for me: I always have several projects on the needles at once, I need something very portable, and I want something inexpensive so I can record ideas that are only just forming and may go nowhere. Mini journals—small pamphlets with 8 pages or so—fit all these criteria. I use university exam blue books, covering them with inspiring pictures I've pulled from magazines and old calendars.

Make it Yours Think about how you work best. Your goal is to be able to review your notes and pick up where you left off no matter how much time has passed. However you choose to keep track of your projects, make sure to include the following information:

✳ Date.
✳ Your initial concept for the garment.
✳ The source of inspiration or color harmony.
✳ Color numbers and names of the yarns used in the swatches. Tape snippets of yarn to the page. ••••
✳ Needle sizes.

DRIVING TO CAMP

My inspiration for this sweater was the scenery on my summer drive to Meg Swansen's Knitting Camp in Wisconsin. I find myself relaxing the closer I get to camp—all those blues and greens are just relaxing colors for me. The more I thought about a warm Fair Isle cardigan to wear during a cold dreary Ohio winter the more those warm relaxing thoughts of Knitting Camp and my drive to Wisconsin spoke to me.

My advice? Just enjoy the process. And don't be afraid to get started. I loved everything about working on my sweater and am very happy with my end result.

To be honest I came up with the idea for this sweater many years ago. My good knitting buddy, Janine, said the best way to design a Fair Isle sweater was to use colors from a picture where the colors were pleasing to you. I told her about the colors on my drive to Wisconsin, and she smiled and asked if I had a picture. I said I had hours of pictures in my head and could choose colors from that. She smiled patiently and said that a picture would make things easier. I forged ahead. I spent hours—more like years—choosing colors based on my memories and swatching away. But I wasn't happy with any of my swatches!

Pictured left to right:

Spindrift #684 Cobalt

Spindrift #134 Blue Danube

Spindrift #812 Prairie

Spindrift #365 Chartreuse

Spindrift #478 Amber

Holly struggled to find the right colors for her sweater until she took a photograph (left). She knit many short speed swatches (below).

Using an inspiration In the summer of 2012 I took Janine's Design Your Own Fair Isle Class. I brought a photo I had taken of the drive to Knitting Camp to work from. To tell you the truth I loved the swatch from those colors more than I had liked any swatch I had done from my color memory over the previous four or five years. Gotta say it: Janine is right. I probably could have stopped right there and enjoyed my little swatch forever but I forged ahead.

The speed swatching was lots of fun. I liked my beginning speed swatches so well I am kind of surprised I didn't just end up making some little pin cushions using those.

Color choices Its hard to explain the progression of my swatches exactly. In the first speed swatch it was all the colors together. Then I grouped them into the blues and then the greens. I wanted to add an unexpected color and for some reason I ended up with orange—I thought of it as a very dark yellow, like the line down the center of the road. I just liked it with the greens. The process of deciding whether to go from light to dark or dark to light was just trial and error. In fact, one of the hardest parts was just deciding to stop swatching and get on with knitting the sweater.

Working with bands I gravitate toward multiple-pattern sweaters with peerie bands as opposed to allover patterns, so those are the motifs I chose. Choosing the patterns themselves was difficult for me—I guess I like them all. I took my motifs from Alice Starmore's *Charts for Colour Knitting*, although I ended up lengthening the blue pattern to make it a few rows taller. I wanted the largest pattern to be in the green family and the smaller pattern to be in the blue. I also envisioned that the peerie pattern would reflect the highway so it would be gray. For the sweater design, I knew that I wanted a modified drop-shoulder cardigan and I also knew that I didn't want especially wide sleeves. I stuck to that plan and love the fit of my sweater. ❖

LATVIAN FOREST CARDIGAN

My inspiration photo was torn from a *Condé Nast Traveler* magazine article on Budapest's Gellért Baths (January 2011). Teal is my favorite color, and the picture showed teals and turquoises with golden browns and lavender. I thought it was an interesting combination of colors. Color families were aqua green, orange-yellow, and blue-violet.

I wanted a cardigan with an allover pattern and a distinctive border along the bottom edge of the sweater. I also wanted to incorporate Latvian motifs in the sweater since Latvian knitting is a special focus of mine. In my mini journal, I wrote, "Why—the challenge of designing with heathered colors using Latvian overall design, border at bottom, the beauty of Fair Isle garments."

My overall vision did not change through the design process, but the details of achieving it changed. The biggest challenge was the bottom border—choosing which colors and motif to use so that the border was distinct from the overall pattern but still flowed and worked with the overall without seeming like it was out of place.

Swatching for Success From first speed swatch to the final plan I knit 14 separate swatches. The smallest swatch measures just over 1 inch long ("Oh, that's not working!") and the largest is about 6 x 15 inches. To really see what was going on, I felt it was important to have a swatch that was 2 motifs wide by 2 motifs tall. That way I could see what happened within the motif as well as between the motifs and view the colors as they flowed in and back out again. Therefore, once I was close to my final plan, I cast on and worked larger swatches to get a good picture of what the sweater would look like.

The overall motif came from an out-of-print book titled *Latviešu Cimdu Raksti* (*Ornaments in Latvian Gloves and Mittens*), a chart book that was published in the US in 1970 for the Latvian expat community. The border design is a traditional Latvian heathcock tail design that I had used in a previous Latvian mitten.

Building the border The biggest challenge was getting the colors for the border to work with the rest of the design. My original plan was to use golds and purples in the heathcock tail border but the colors in the yellow family were too strong and bright to go with the colors I had chosen for the flow of the overall design. A friend suggested moving away from the golds and purples for the border, and when I let go of that plan, the new plan using the blue-green motif on the brown family background needed just a few tweaks to make it work.

Once the border plan was worked out, the color sequence for the corrugated ribbing went together easily. ❖

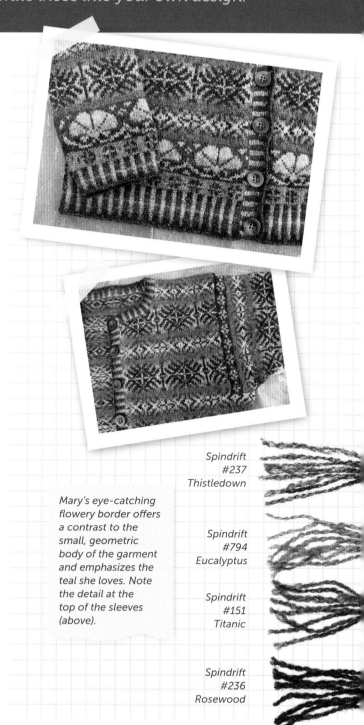

Mary's eye-catching flowery border offers a contrast to the small, geometric body of the garment and emphasizes the teal she loves. Note the detail at the top of the sleeves (above).

Spindrift #237 Thistledown

Spindrift #794 Eucalyptus

Spindrift #151 Titanic

Spindrift #236 Rosewood

Color

* Color in Fair Isle

* Find your colors

* Speed swatching

Hello, Color!

Odds are you don't think you are good with color. Perhaps you think that color-mixing ability is an inborn trait and that you missed out. Well, anyone can learn to use color effectively. In this chapter I'll introduce some general concepts about color use in Fair Isle knitting and then outline several different ways to choose colors for your custom garment.

Color is a large and complicated subject that can seem quite intimidating, but you don't need a degree in art to make lovely color choices. The most important skill is to learn to really *see* color without preconceptions. Sometimes people cannot think of a color unattached to a thing, the way a child draws the sky as blue, for example. But is the sky a simple blue? Or cerulean blue? Azure? Blue-violet? Or are there shades of gray, or white, or deeper blue near the horizon, even a touch of purple or pink?

Color is cultural and individual

There are no absolutes about color. Different cultures find different color combinations pleasing. Each culture arbitrarily places a "grid" over the color spectrum, labels colors, and assigns meaning to them. For example, in many languages there was no linguistic distinction between blue and green.

Artists and physicists have tried to categorize color relationships for centuries. Their color theories can be difficult to understand; remember that color theory is simply an attempt to explain how waves of light translate into what we see. But color also has an emotional aspect that can't be ignored. Learn just enough color theory to help you understand what you are seeing and to help you solve problems.

The bottom line is that we cannot reduce color to a formula and get an exciting result. That's good news, but it also means that there is no one surefire formula for creating your Fair Isle design.

Colorful terms

When I talk about color use I'll be using a few words that you might not be familiar with:

Value: how dark or light something appears—a very important concept in Fair Isle knitting.

Tint: the pure color plus white.

Shade: the pure color plus black.

Tone: gray added to any form of the color—pure, tint, or shade.

Color family: the pure color plus tints, shades, and tones.

Complements: colors that sit opposite each other on the color wheel.

Analogous colors: colors that sit beside each other on the color wheel.

How to determine value in yarns

A number of tools are available to help you determine value:

✳ Take a black and white photograph of your yarns with your phone or digital camera.

✳ Place the yarns on a photocopier or scanner —use a "High Quality" setting to show the finer variations. And do keep track of which ball you set where on the scanner bed!

✳ View the yarn through red and green mylar films, which filter out the distractions of color.

✳ Squint! Your eyes are excellent tools—if you squint, the information about color is suppressed a bit.

The best test for value is to swatch! It's hard to accurately determine the value of the yarn when it is in the ball, especially when you are working with heathers and tweeds. Once you make the swatch, you'll know!

Here is a dark-to-light gradation within a single color family (left). The same swatch is shown in black and white (right) to demonstrate the values more clearly.

These values move from dark to light through several color families.

Color in Fair Isle Knitting

Fair Isle designs have a unique way of arranging colors that is instantly recognizable. This distinctive color use relies on three elements: value gradations, mirroring, and value contrast to produce a three-dimensional effect.

1 VALUE GRADATIONS Gradations, ombré, sequences —it doesn't matter what we call them—are at the core of what makes Fair Isle knitting so beguiling. In a gradation colors are arranged by value (how dark or light they appear) so that they move from light to dark (or vice versa). There's something about gradients that is fundamentally appealing .

The value movement in Fair Isle design can be very smooth, or it can be composed of more obvious value steps. It can involve 10 colors or 3. The important point is that the sequence holds together visually.

The values can move from lightest light to darkest dark, or they can be more subtle, moving from white to a medium beige, for example.

You can move from one color family to another within a value sequence. Even though the sequence might move through several color families they all seem to fit together when the values are controlled.

2 MIRRORING TIED TO THE MOTIF Fair Isle designs are generally symmetrical, that is, the pattern moves into a center row and then flips so that the motif mirrors itself.

Color gradations are used the same way: they sequence to the center row of the motif and then the sequences reverses out of the center row.

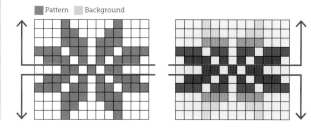

Possible Value Arrangements

In Fair Isle design, the number of color combinations is limitless, but there are only a limited number of ways to arrange the value gradations:

Simple A single color pattern and background

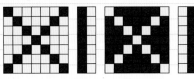

A Bit More Complex

A single color pattern and shifting color background (left). A shifting color pattern and single color background (right).

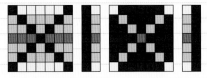

Complex

Both the pattern and the background have gradations. There are 4 possible ways to arrange the sequences.

Parallel values The background shifts from dark to light while the pattern shifts from dark to light (left). The background shifts from light to dark while the pattern shifts from light to dark (right

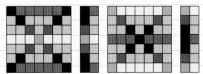

Opposing values The background shifts dark to light while the pattern shifts from light to dark (left).The background shifts light to dark while the pattern shifts from dark to light (right).

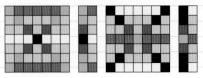

A pop color at the very center of the motif highlights the design's turn point. This center color is often bright, but sometimes it is as subtle as a lighter or darker shade of the color that lies on each side of it. (More about pop colors in *Motifs*.)

3 VALUE CONTRAST When you combine value gradations with motifs you have to keep in mind value contrast *between* the pattern and the background.

At times patterns show up strongly against the background; sometimes they nearly disappear. Blurring occurs naturally when you work with opposing value gradations—the medium values will cross at some point. No matter how different in saturation or brightness if the values are the same the design will not show up. This is not a problem. The human eye is drawn to areas of ambiguity, and this blurriness is one of the charms of Fair Isle color usage.

Your job is to make sure the motif is not broken apart when pattern and background values get close. Therefore, if the values of your pattern and background are fairly close you will want to choose patterns that are visually heavy and predictable. If your values have a high contrast, however, you might choose light, asymmetric patterns (more on this in *Motifs*).

Don't panic

In the abstract, this might seem overwhelming. But the design process is very hands on—there's nothing abstract about it. When you have your colors in front of you and begin to line them up into sequences, these concepts will begin to make sense.

There is only so much you can anticipate—the process of swatching will reveal whether you've made the right choices. This is a very active process. Allow yourself to feel some level of doubt at each stage of choosing your colors. Knitting the swatches will give you the information you need.

Same Concepts in Knitting

How do these three principles—value gradation, mirroring, and value contrast—translate into knitting? These examples show some of the ways you can arrange nine colors—five in the pattern and four in the background

1. Here is the yarn, arranged in two value sequences. Each sample is knit with the same sequence of colors.

2. Solid pattern/solid background. The motif stands out clearly because there is a strong value contrast between the pattern and the background.

3. Solid pattern/gradated background. Notice how smooth the value gradation is—it's OK to have rougher transitions. The motif stands out clearly because the pattern is much darker than every color in the background.

4. Gradated pattern/solid background. This time the pattern uses the value sequence. The outer edges of the pattern are faint but visible against the background.

5. Gradated pattern and background: parallel value movement. Things are getting more interesting! The motif is still readable because at every step of the gradation the pattern remains darker than the background.

6. Gradated pattern and background: opposing value movement. The center of the motif disappears because the values of the motif and the background are too close. The colors would have to be re-arranged to avoid this problem.

Golden Yellow

#182 Buttercup

#375 Flax

#389 Gold

#289 Gold

#1160 Scotch Broom

#230 Yellow Ochre

#429 Old Gold

#246 Wren

Blue-Violet

#1390 Highland Mist

#175 Twilight

#615 Hyacinth

#628 Parma

#629 Lupin

Color Families

In order to get the value sequences you need for your design you need to understand the concept of color families.

When you look at a color wheel the first thing you notice is the saturated form of the color. These colors are the hues that pop to mind when you think of, say, green or red. But a color family includes all the other forms of the color: the tints, shades, tones, murky browns, tweeds (a base color with flecks of different colors), and heathers (yarns with mixed colors, often white or grays).

The yarn examples here show three different color families in Jamieson Shetland Spindrift yarn. If your design calls for Blue-Violet, you can use any of these yarns depending on what effect you are trying to achieve. There is a big difference between Hyacinth (a tint), Twilight (a tweed), and Highland Mist (a toned heather)—but they are all members of the same family.

Some families can surprise The Blue-Violet family doesn't reveal any surprises (blue families are consistent throughout), but the Golden Yellow and the Chartreuse families might. When you add black to colors with yellow in them, you get a form of olive.

So if your design requires Chartreuse, you can use Earth or Birch; you don't have to include a bright chartreuse in your sweater.

You want to gather a range of values from each family because you don't know what will be useful as you work on your design. Refrain from pre-judging colors. You might say that you hate tints, or muddy colors, or brights, but they might be just the color you need for your design.

#294 Blueberry

#710 Gentian

Chartreuse

#140 Rye

#365 Chartreuse

#791 Pistachio

#789 Marjoram

#226 Thyme

#998 Autumn

#252 Birch

#235 Grouse

#227 Earth

Find Your Colors

The question on your mind—what is probably making you most anxious—is this: How do I choose colors that will look good together? Maybe you don't think you are good with color or you've tried to design your own Fair Isle and weren't successful.

Although some people would seem to have an innate sense of color that translates seamlessly to Fair Isle colorwork, this sure mastery is generally the result of lots of experimentation. Intellectual understanding of color relationships is helpful, but Fair Isle color use demands experiential work.

Adults have trouble with this concept—they want to understand and then proceed ahead perfectly. Remember: your mastery of this art will be the result of knitting lots of swatches.

Choosing colors for stranded designs is a two-step process

1. Determine the color families you want to work with.

2. Find the yarns within those color families that will make the design work.

How do you make these decisions if you aren't confident in your ability to choose colors? There are three different methods that can help guide your choices:

● Find a source of inspiration.

● Turn to color theory.

● Trust your instinct.

3-IN-1 COLOR TOOL

My understanding of color relationships and my ability to identify color families solidified when I was introduced to the 24-color color wheel. I could not find where my yarns fit on a 12-color wheel—there just wasn't enough information for my untrained eyes to figure out what I was looking at. I use Joen Wolfrom's *Ultimate 3-in-1 Color Tool* for all my color work.

FROM FLAT WHEEL TO 3-DIMENSIONAL YARN

When you view color on a wheel the printed color is flat and continuous, but fiber behaves differently. Yarn is a soft, three-dimensional, multi-hued substance. Start with a wheel, but let your swatching guide you in creating color families for your design.

Labels can be deceiving, too. While yarn companies often market their wares with wonderful color names like "lime" and "ochre," the color truth in knitting comes from how the yarns behave together in your swatch, not from assigned color name.

A Colorful Cap in Six Steps

THE CHANGEABLE WEATHER of northern New Mexico in October is always inspirational! I was taken by this photo in particular and decided to base a design—the October Storm Cap—on it by following the steps outlined in this chapter.

Step One: Identify the color families in the inspiration. Focusing on one color at a time, I move the color wheel or *3-in-1 Color Tool* (a 24-color family wheel) across the photo, searching for a general impression of color, not specific forms of the color. I determined that the main color families were golden yellow, chartreuse, blue, and blue-violet.

Step Two: Gather yarns in those color families. I find as many as I can, even colors I don't like. For Fair Isle designs we need lights and darks, brights and dulls, maybe some murky shades that incorporate the color family.

When searching for colors I might take some from nearby color families if I need their values—value is more important than color.

Step Three: Line up and speed swatch the yarns. I tested different value arrangements of these yarns—this was my favorite. Notice the high value contrast between the two columns at each end; I don't like high contrast areas, but Fair Isle designs need them.

Step Four: Decide on a motif. Because the colors seemed to flow so well I chose an allover contiguous pattern (as opposed to a banded pattern).

Step Five: Swatch the colors with the motif. Rather than swatching I made a hat. If you are feeling pretty confident, knitting a cap doesn't take much longer than knitting a motif swatch—and you have a hat! Templates for caps and tams are in *Odds & Ends*.

615 Hyacinth

617 Lavender

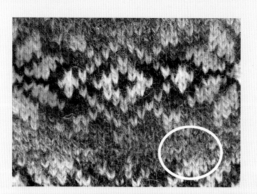

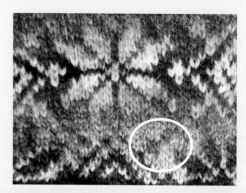

Step Six: Analyze the motif swatch. I loved how this turned out, but there was one area I thought could be improved (above, left). I added two more colors to smooth out the value transitions: Jamieson Shetland Spindrift 617 Lavender and 615 Hyacinth (new swatch on right). ❖

Using a visual source of inspiration is an excellent way to choose your colors. The inspiration is a starting point—your garment might look very different.

WORK FROM A COLOR INSPIRATION

Using a source of inspiration—a photograph, a painting, a textile, a piece of pottery—is an excellent way to pin down color families that will work well together. If you like the inspiration you will like your color combination.

I strongly recommend this method if you are just starting out. An inspiring photo or graphic may lead to color combinations you might not have come up with on your own, and you will develop a deeper understanding of how colors work together. The resulting designs will prove to be complex and very personal.

Sources of inspiration

Paintings and textiles can be easier to work from than photographs because the artist has already reduced the number of color families.

The natural world knows no color boundaries so photos of nature scenes are difficult. If you are drawn to a picture of a mountain meadow, for example, pick the three or four most prominent color families rather than trying to handle twelve.

Accurate color memory is notoriously rare. Trust me: you will be happier if you use a photo rather than your memory.

Identify the families

Which color families are in your inspiration? Working one color at a time, pull out a color tool or wheel and run it across the picture, trying to determine which family best describes it. If you have trouble make a simple mask to help you see more clearly, as shown in the upper left example.

It takes some practice to learn to think in terms of color families. Don't try to find the specific form of the color—the exact toned tint, for example—that is in your inspiration. Look for the family and write it in your mini journal.

Note the proportions in your inspiration and the form that the colors in it come in. You might want to keep most of your colors muted, for example, if that is what drew you to your inspiration.

Follow Color Theory

You can use color theory to make your color family decisions.

- Pick a color family that you like or find a ball of yarn you like, and find out where it fits on the color wheel. Every other color decision stems from this one.

- Check out the back of the color wheel, where you will find a few suggestions for natural color harmonies. Remember that the color harmonies are shown with the colors in their saturated forms; therefore, these combinations might seem too bright to your eye.

- Keep in mind that you are looking for color *families*. The yarns you choose from within those families can be light or dark or grayed or heathered.

Simple harmonies

The fewer the color families involved, the easier it is to design a Fair Isle. The triadic, analogous, and split-complementary harmonies are particularly easy to work with. You can make any color work well with another by finding a harmony that includes them both and adding the other suggested color families.

Pop colors

Color theory can help you identify pop colors, too (more about pop colors on page 68). If you can't figure out which color will make your design sing, check the color wheel for complements.

Color Groupings on the Wheel

In addition to complements (colors directly across from each other on the color wheel), there are a number of natural harmonies that can guide your decisions. If you don't feel confident, try the simpler harmonies. On the other hand, jump in and play with complexity!

Triad
three color familes evenly spaced around the wheel.

Analogous
colors that are next to each other on the wheel.

Split-complementary
using two colors adjacent to their complement.

Tetrad
four colors arranged into two complementary pairs.

Hexad
three pairs of complementary colors that are equidistant from one another.

Double triad
two trios of hues equidistant on the wheel.

Rainforest Vest

I STARTED WITH a color called Grouse, a deep deep shade of chartreuse. I decided to work with complementary color families, so I turned to the color wheel to find the complement of chartreuse: red-violet.

Both color families are used in the background and the pattern; the pattern is always darker than the background. A single line of Mist works as a subtle pop color.

MOTIF I found a Komi mitten band in Charlene Schurch's *Marvelous Mittens*. I photocopied it a few times, cut out the motifs, and tried placing them in different relationships until I found one that would work for an allover pattern.

I played around with the value sequences, but eventually decided on a parallel value movement, with the motif being always darker than the background.

GARMENT FEATURES I started with a purl-when-you-can patterned rib. The shoulders were formed using the shaped shoulders in the round technique and were joined with a 3-needle I-cord bind off. The armholes were edged with I-cord as well. The shawl collar and front bands were knit in moss stitch out of a single strand of yarn; this feels a little flimsy in relation to the vest itself. Next time I would use the yarn doubled to give it more heft.

BROWN When complements are used in roughly 50/50 amounts, they will turn into brown when viewed at a distance. The result is that, although the vest looks bright up close, it gives a muted impression. ❖

Celtic Knot Sweater

I STARTED BY PICKING the body color, a lovely red-violet called Loganberry. Sometimes I start a yoke sweater without knowing how I will design the yoke: knitting the body and sleeves is enjoyably mindless and leaves a lot of time to plot colors and pattern.

SPEED SWATCHING I decided to use a triadic harmony so I pulled colors from the other color families in the triad: yellow-orange and blue-green. I then made quick speed and motif swatches. Because each band was separate I could play a little, ready to rip if necessary.

SWIRLING PATTERNS It was hard to choose from all the Celtic knot patterns in Co Spinhoven's *Celtic Charted Designs*. I based my decisions on the height limits of the yoke. These asymmetrical patterns need a lot of value contrast to hold together visually. ❖

I played with some different sequence arrangements—opposing values (upper half of speed swatch at left) and parallel values (lower half of speed swatch)—before adding colors to the motifs.

Unexpected color combinations on a yarn shop's shelf, a snippet of poetry, a view that evokes a feeling—keep your heart open.

WORK FROM INSTINCT

After you've made a few designs you will begin to understand how to combine colors intuitively. With your newfound confidence you might even feel ready to trust your instincts.

Maybe you dream of a pink sweater. Or one that captures the mood of a remembered winter day. A poem might ask to be reflected in yarn. Or you might find that you are inspired by a random pairing of colors that you see on a yarn shop's shelves. You wouldn't have thought to put these colors together, but suddenly your imagination is captured. Take notes, using specific and descriptive words to help you remember.

The most challenging aspect of working from instinct is finding the colors that will make the combination sing. Take advantage of the color harmony information on your color wheel to add some spark to your design.

You'll still choose your yarns as if you were working from an inspiration or a color wheel: find some colors you like and then identify the color families that they belong to in order to find the values that you need for Fair Isle color work.

Speed Swatch for Color

No matter which method you used to determine the color families you will work with—color inspiration, color theory, or instinct—Feral Rule #3 says: You cannot tell whether colors will work together unless you swatch. There are no exceptions to this rule!

Swatching is time consuming and trying to swatch colors *and* motifs at the same time takes forever. To make the process more efficient, start with swatching for color only.

This "speed swatch for color"—a simple diagonal pattern in which the colors change at regular intervals—accomplishes several goals at once:

- The swatch allows you to see which colors work together and which need to be tossed.

- The swatch shows which colors or values might be missing in your collection.

- You see whether your value sequences are correct.

- The swatch hints at what kind of motifs might work best with your colors.

- The swatch shows whether the feeling of the colors knit together is what you were aiming for.

Gather a Palette of Yarns

You've identified your color families. Now the fun begins: you will choose yarns from those color families to build your value sequences.

Starting with a single color family, use your yarn library or color cards to identify all the available yarns in that family. (It is easiest to work with one color family at a time.) Keep your color wheel in front of you.

Look for the entire range of the family: lights, darks, heathers, bright, dull, browns with undertones in your family. Some color families will be well represented in the yarn line you have chosen to work with; others will consist of just two or three yarns.

This process is much easier if you have lots of yarns at your fingertips. If you are working from a color card or the internet, make copious notes as you identify colors

Dyeing your own yarn

No matter how many yarn colors are available, there inevitably comes a moment when you can't find the perfect color or value you want for your design!

When you dye your own yarn, you are like an artist mixing the exact colors needed for her painting. Which means you have an infinity of colors to choose from.

While this might sound appealing, it takes only a few minutes of wrestling with your design to realize that infinite possibilities can also be a real headache.

On the plus side...
- ✳ You can fill in gaps in commercial color offerings.
- ✳ You can get the exact hue you want.
- ✳ You can get the exact value you want.

On the other hand...
- ✳ You have too many choices, which can be paralyzing.
- ✳ You can't get tweeds or heathers unless you also blend and spin your own yarn.

How to make a flat swatch

1. Cast on, using a circular needle.
2. Break off the yarn, leaving a 3-4" tail.
3. Push the knitting back to the right-hand end of the needle.
4. Knit to the end.
5. Break off the yarns, leaving 3-4" long tails.
6. Push the knitting back to the right-hand end of the needle and begin again.
7. Every two rows knot the 4 ends together snugly at each side of the swatch.

With this method you are always knitting with the right side of the work facing you, using the needles you plan to use for your project.

that fit your families. Try scanning the color card or downloading photos of the yarns; print these pictures at the highest possible print quality—they will be a poor substitute for the yarns themselves, but they will help in a pinch as you move to the next step.

If you are confused, note that mills often dye their yarns in natural sequences—if you stumble on one of these take advantage of it. Notice how yarns are arranged on the color cards; companies often organize the cards by color family. But keep your eyes open for additional possibilities.

Now, do the same thing for each of the other color families you've identified.

Build Your Color Sequences

Now you have a pile of yarns in front of you, or perhaps a pile of yarn printouts.

Begin with a single value gradation. This could have 3 or 4 or 5 or any number of colors in it, depending on the choices in front of you. Don't just look at your collection of colors and say to yourself, "Well, I'll use that one first and then this one...." Place them in value order in front of you. Adults tend to want to solve problems intellectually, so pretend that you are a child—pick up the yarns, move them around, set them in place, play.

Build a second value gradation. When you are satisfied with the first sequence, make another one with the same number of colors right beside it. Squint. Does it look like the pattern would show up against the background? What happens if you turn one of the gradations upside down?

Feeling Overwhelmed?

Try making a single gradation and placing a solid color with it, making sure that the solid is darker than the darkest color in the sequence, or lighter as the case may be. Excellent designs can come out of simplified color arrangements!

While building your sequences you might have noticed gaps in your yarn collection. Go back to the color card looking to fill these gaps—you might have to stray out of your color family to find the value you need.

Knit Your Speed Swatch

Order your yarn and follow the instructions in the sidebar to knit a speed swatch with the sequences you built.

Analyze the Speed Swatch

Look at your first swatch critically. Ask yourself:

- Do any of these colors not fit, that is, did you misread the color family for any yarn?

- Did these colors go flat? Many of the yarns used for Fair Isle knitting are tones and become more gray when combined with other tones.

- Are there some color combinations that are surprisingly nice?

- Did you get the value sequencing correct? Hard to tell until you swatch. Moving from color family A to color family B and back to color family A in a sequence can disrupt the sequence visually even if the values themselves are correct.

- Are any important colors missing?

- Is there enough value difference between the sequences for a pattern to show up? (There is usually an area where there isn't enough value contrast, especially when you are working with opposing values—these can be kept apart in the motif swatch.)

- Does the overall feel reflect what you liked about the inspiration?

- Does the swatch overall look unbalanced—too much of one color family?

- You might not like the areas with the highest contrast, but don't be hasty in dismissing them: they are necessary in the design.

Maybe you fell into a lovely combination of colors, but it is more likely that you will need to do several more speed swatches, tweaking a little here and there to realize your vision. Try opposing values. Try a solid with a gradation. Try parallel values. Reduce the number of colors you are working with. Expand them. The colors you have before you offer an infinite number of possibilities. Play with different combinations.

LIMITATIONS

This speed swatch for color has two limitations: It shows the same amount of each color and it is very small. Your motif swatches will reveal more about how the colors work together —the speed swatch for color simply points you in the right direction and helps eliminate colors that won't work.

When you are generally happy with your speed swatches, it is time to swatch your colors in a motif.

HOW TO KNIT A SPEED SWATCH IN FIVE STEPS

The speed swatch for color is a tool to help you understand how your colors work together.

1. From your yarn families create two sequences of equal numbers of colors that might work together. Decide how you want to arrange them based on the options shown on page 28. By "work" I mean there should be enough value contrast between the two sequences that a pattern would show up. If you don't feel confident, use a solid color plus a sequence.

If you are planning to make a banded sweater, you can make short sequences of three or four colors. If you want to make an allover contiguous design you can make your sequences as long as possible.

2. Fill in the speed swatch chart on page 138, using as many rows as you need (see page 50 on preparing charts). By the time you run out of rows, you should be able to swatch without looking at a chart.

3. Cast on 20 stitches with the first color in column A and follow the chart (row one of the chart is the cast-on row). Don't bind off when you have finished.

4. Analyze your swatch.

5. Knit a couple of rows of a single color, rearrange your colors, and try another speed swatch. When you find one that you like, try mirroring the colors—read about pop colors on page 68 and add one to your speed swatch, or leave it out for now.

In *Odds & Ends* you will find speed swatch charts, but very quickly you will find that you won't need one. Learning to read your knitting rather than a chart is an important skill that you can develop with practice.

Ways to develop color confidence

Choose a photograph or a painting and try to identify the colors in it—look for the small touch of unexpected color, for example, in the center of a tulip or the cobalt blue piping on the burgundy and saffron monk's robe. Analyze paintings that catch your attention.

When you are taking a walk, pause to name the colors you see as accurately as possible. For example, when looking at a leaf, don't just think "green." Yellow-green? Tinge of pink? Blue-green?

Learn some basic color theory. The back of most color wheels offers suggestions about successful color harmonies. Note that any two colors can be made to work together if you add other moderating color families—the old rules about colors that shouldn't be used together fly right out the window!

Mix paints to make tints, shades, and tones. Move from one color family to another. Create a color wheel from three primaries.

Analyze a Fair Isle design you like. Find out where the colors the designer chose fall on the color wheel. Imagine what would happen if you shifted the colors 90° around the wheel.

Buy a coloring book and a set of colored pencils. Plunge in.

Play with your yarn collection. Arrange the yarns in color family groups. Now try arranging them by value. Revel in all the colors. Toss them all together and see if some interesting color connections happen, and then try to verbalize why they work. Find colors that don't look good together and figure out why. Make pointless speed swatches. Grab any 10 colors and see if you can make them work together.

Fun Shortcuts

Perhaps this discussion of value sequencing and mirroring and contrast has you feeling a bit deflated. Here are two fun alternatives to all that planning: Faux (false) Fair Isle and Magic Ball. Both of these methods let you move on automatic pilot once you've chosen your yarn. It's best to use strong geometric motifs with these methods because you don't have much control over your value contrasts.

Notice that without value sequencing or mirroring you lose the three-dimensional effect of purposefully placed values that is a hallmark of true Fair Isle.

Faux Fair Isle

Choose a yarn that has long color repeats, such as Kauni, and a solid color for your project (or another color-changing yarn). The trick is to use a contrasting color that is much darker than the darkest color in the multicolor yarn or one that is much lighter than the lightest color. If you reach an area with inadequate value contrast, break off the yarn, remove the problem color, and continue on.

Magic Ball

In magic ball knitting you create your own long color repeats by knotting together lengths of different colors. Your magic ball is most effective if you sequence your values as you build your ball.

Two magic balls—one dark and one light—were used in this version of the Inspira Cowl *by Graphica.*

To Do

1 Decide whether you will work from an inspiration, color theory, or instinct.

2 Determine which color families you will be working with.

3 Choose yarns from those color families. Be sure to include tints, shades, tones, heathers, tweeds, and muddy complements to expand your value range.

4 Order any colors you think you might need.

5 Line your yarn up in two value gradations.

6 Knit a speed swatch (don't bind off yet!).

7 Analyze your speed swatch. Remember: you are learning about your colors, how they react in different situations. If your confidence is plummeting, try simplifying your color story for your next swatch.

8 Repeat steps 5–7 until you are satisfied. Sometimes your colors will fall into place right away, at other times it takes several attempts to get two gradations that work well together.

To Explore

USING COLOR IN FAIR ISLE
The Art of Fair Isle Knitting by Ann Feitelson.
The best discussion of color use in Fair Isle knitting, with a focus on value sequences and how they function.

How to Select Color Palettes for Knitting and Other Fiber Arts by Nancy Shroyer.
Guidance for using color theory for designing knitwear.

Color Works by Deb Menz.
Taking color from theory to practice! Excellent reference by an expert in color and fiber, although not specifically about Fair Isle knitting.

ABOUT COLOR IN GENERAL
Color Play, second edition by Joen Wolfrom.
Thorough and inspirational exploration of color families and harmonies.

The Secret Language of Color by Joan Eckstut and Arielle Eckstut.
An excellent and readable introduction to color in general: specific hues as well as how color manifests itself in the physical world around us.

To Inspire

In order to use color effectively, it is necessary to recognize that color deceives continually. — **JOSEPH ALBERS**

GOAT ROCK V-NECK PULLOVER

My sweater was inspired by Goat Rock Beach in the Sonoma Headlands. The colors and textures of the headlands move me deeply. This particular beach, Goat Rock, is where the Russian River meets the Pacific Ocean. It's just magical to me.

My advice? You can make your first project as big or small a deal as you want. You can focus on color play, or structure, or both. You can be as daring or conservative as you're comfortable with. Since it's about color, choose a structure you're comfortable with and work in it.

My vision changed a lot while designing this sweater! Colors that I initially thought would be most prominent didn't need to be. I think the project started with about 9 more colors than it ultimately contains. I really thought white or very pale grey would be included, but they just didn't work at all in the body of the sweater. I did use a single row of light grey in the cuffs and collar band.

Open mind I actually love to swatch, so that was one of the best parts. You get to play with all the colors you think you need and then make some critical decisions about what is, and isn't, necessary. It requires you to have an open mind and to let go of preconceptions. If you trust the colors they will tell your story. You just need to not let your frontal lobe get in the way.

Choosing a motif The main motif is from Co Spinhoven's _Celtic Charted Designs_ with a slight modification or two. The swirls on the top portion of the motif represent the horns of a ram, and the swirls on the bottom the waves of the water. The signature and date I just did myself. There isn't a motif to the bands, just colorwork.

Challenges Inconsistent gauge and sizing were my biggest challenges. I knitted several inches before I got consistent gauge and then had to re-knit to make it actually fit. Of course, that meant rearranging motifs so they'd work out, too. Time management was also an issue. I always have too much going on to devote as much time as I wish I could to get it done sooner.

The actual construction was pretty straightforward and easy. Once the colors were worked out it was just total fun to build each row on to the next.

Trust the colors I imagine that for some people focusing on just one of these might be sufficient. Most importantly, let go of preconceptions. You have to trust the colors. Your eyes and brain can fool you, but the colors will speak for themselves.

Just enjoy the ride. Its definitely an "E" ticket! ❖

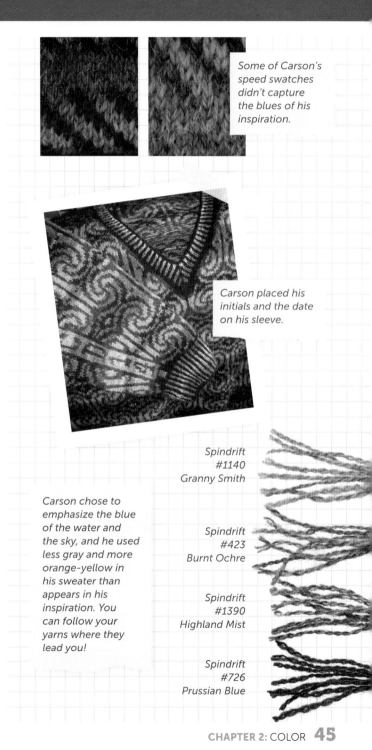

Some of Carson's speed swatches didn't capture the blues of his inspiration.

Carson placed his initials and the date on his sleeve.

Carson chose to emphasize the blue of the water and the sky, and he used less gray and more orange-yellow in his sweater than appears in his inspiration. You can follow your yarns where they lead you!

Spindrift
#1140
Granny Smith

Spindrift
#423
Burnt Ochre

Spindrift
#1390
Highland Mist

Spindrift
#726
Prussian Blue

Sinaguan Sweater

The inspiration piece for my Fair Isle sweater was a photo in *Arizona Highways* magazine. The picture highlighted Montezuma Castle, framed by the limbs of a tree in the Arizona desert (David Muench, *Arizona Highways*, August 2011). The colors in this piece spoke to me: the limestone cliffs that form the castle are my favorite color—salmon. And the bark of the tree in the foreground of the photo is comprised of blues, red-violets, dark blue-violets, and oranges.

Before I started playing with color I selected the pattern I was planning to use. Ultimately I chose a traditional Estonian pattern that I found in a mitten book. The pattern repeat was 30 stitches. There was one round of the pattern in which I had to tack down my floats as they were longer than one inch. I knew I was going to make a traditional pullover sweater as I am always cold!

Speed swatching The process of speed swatching and establishing the value sequences of both the background and pattern colors was a challenging experience! It took me quite some time to get the colors and values worked out to my liking. I initially thought that the background would consist of the cool hues of the tree, the

blues and violets, and the pattern would be the salmon limestone colors. When swatched, the final result was not pleasing; in fact, it seemed rather boring so I decided to flip the background and the pattern colors. The final design started to take shape.

The last key design decision involved selecting the "poison" colors or turning points in the centers of the pattern repeats. The red-violet taken from the bark in the photo worked great in the middle of the cool, blue background colors. I had wanted to incorporate the orange that was part of the bark of the tree here, but I discovered I needed to maintain warm colors in the background and cool ones in the pattern stitches. Introducing a warm hue as the center of the cool pattern colors was not effective.

Sweater construction After all that prep work, the actual knitting of the sweater was easy and fun. If you have never knit a Fair Isle sweater, it is probably best to knit one or two as a blind follower to understand the general construction. I started by following some Alice Starmore patterns blindly. This helped me greatly to understand the traditional construction of a Fair Isle sweater and also got me thinking about color and value.

The biggest challenge of this project for me was approximating the "feel" of the photo inspiration. Another challenge was learning to honor my "gut" reaction to the swatch instead of overriding it with my thoughts about what "should" be right or what "should" work. A great life lesson!

There is nothing about this process that is really difficult—due in great part to the step-by-step method that Janine has developed. Patience with the swatching process is a necessity! As long has I broke the design process down into small steps and just focused on one swatch as my goal, I found the project less overwhelming.

Break down the process I would encourage knitters to break the job down into manageable segments, as Janine suggests. Stay with the speed swatches until you feel you have a good progression of hues and values. Then move on to swatching using your pattern motif. Fine tune over and over again until you are satisfied.

If you are into speed and "getting things done," have another easy project going at the same time so you can feel you are accomplishing something. Sometimes you just need to step away from the process for a bit, especially if your swatches are not working. The down time allows you to see another way. ❖

Pictured left to right:
Spindrift #578 Rust
Spindrift #232 Blue Lovat
Spindrift #478 Amber
Spindrift #130 Sky

Sandy made many swatches to find a colorway that evoked the feel of her inspiration.

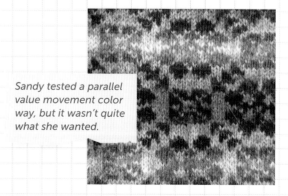

Sandy tested a parallel value movement color way, but it wasn't quite what she wanted.

MOTIFS

* HOW TO CHART

* FINDING MOTIFS

* COMBINING MOTIFS

* ADDING COLOR

Playing With Pattern

From Color to Chart to Knit

The origins of a knitted motif: *Choose your colors, add them to a motif, and knit a swatch.*

You've been playing with your colors and you probably have a pretty good idea of how they can work together. Now you are faced with the infinite possibilities of motif choices!

Start by reviewing your project notes. Remember that you are taking this one step at a time: first you will choose your motif, then you will add your colors to the motif. However, before talking about types of motifs and how to design with them, let's discuss working with charts.

Making Charts

When you evaluate published Fair Isle patterns you will notice that the charts can be formatted in a number of different ways, some of which are extremely hard to decipher. I recommend a specific way of charting when you are designing your own patterns for two reasons:

● It is easy to change colors while working out the design.

● The pattern is crystal clear.

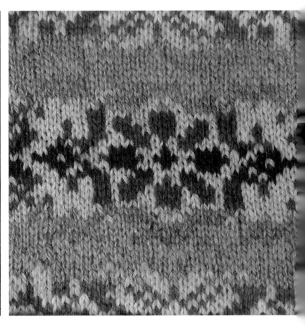

Row	Pattern		Background	
45			Cocoa	1
43	Buttermilk	3(5)		
41			Petrol	4
39	Flax	4		
36			Lunar	5
35	Cashew	4		
32			Seabright	4
31	Burnt Ochre	4		
28			Aqua	4
27	Old Gold	4		
24			China Blue	4
23			Mint	1
20	Olive	7		
19			China Blue	4
16	Old Gold	4		
15			Aqua	4
12	Burnt Ochre	4		
11			Seabright	4
8	Cashew	4		
6			Lunar	5
4	Flax	4		
2			Petrol	4
1	Buttermilk	3(5)	Cocoa	1

The pattern stitches are the dark squares; the background stitches are white. It doesn't matter that the actual design might be a light pattern on a dark background—by consistently charting this way, I know that the dark squares will be knit with my stitch-dominant hand (my left hand) and I don't have to think about it. I can see at a glance what the pattern should look like.

Colors to the side

The colors are shown alongside the chart rather than using symbols or colors in the chart itself because the chart remains quite clear and readable in simple black-and-white. Often our yarn colors look so similar that it is hard to tell which color is called for when viewing a colored chart, and symbols can obscure the motif, causing mistakes when knitting.

In Fair Isle knitting you choose your colors at the start of the round, so you don't need to make any decisions after the round has begun. I put the number of rounds of each color beside the color name to help keep track.

The process of adding colors to a chart involves a lot of changes—using pencil to call out the colors alongside the chart is very practical because it is so flexible.

Charting for pattern

When setting up the chart, how do you know which stitches are the pattern stitches and which the background? If you are unsure, think about what you want to emphasize about the motif and make that the pattern. You might have to flip a coin for some geometric motifs.

WORKING WITH CHARTS

As you knit you will want to mark the rows as you complete them. There are a number of tools to help you keep track: highlighter tape, highlighter pens, magnetic holders, computer apps such as knitCompanion®, or simple light pencil marks. The goal is to show that you've knit the row without obscuring the pattern so that you can orient yourself while knitting.

ELECTRONIC VS. PAPER CHARTING

Fair Isle charts are best created in black and white. Bright, multicolored charts are fantastic fun to look at, but your swatch is the place where working color decisions really get made. Even in black and white there are many roads to charting...

Dedicated programs The ability to duplicate, cut, paste, and rotate with just a few clicks is very useful and can help you visualize alternatives quickly. There are many specialized charting programs such as Stitch Painter® and EnvisioKnit®. Guidance can be found on knitter forums like Ravelry.com.

Spreadsheet apps If you already use Microsoft Excel® or Apple Numbers®, consider creating a grid by setting up .25-inch columns. Assign a symbol a solid color to fill the grid squares.

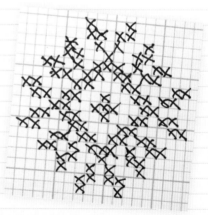

Pencil and paper You don't need a computer, though. Working on paper can help you feel connected to the process of making the garment in fiber. Use colored pencils if you'd like.

The planning paper you'll find at the end of this book along with a copier, a pair of scissors, pencils with erasers, and a roll of scotch tape are all the tools you need to make a great design.

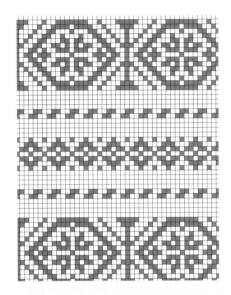

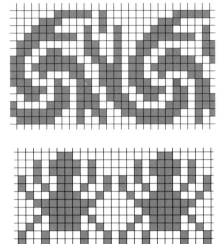

Symmetrical bands: *Each band of patterns is separate; repetition and contrast create a larger rhythm.*

Symmetrical allover contiguous: *Unbroken patterns like these can be used on all or part of the garment.*

Asymmetrical: *Non-symmetrical patterns range from isolated figurative motifs to repetitive connected designs.*

Types of Motifs

Motifs can be generally classified into three categories:

Symmetrical bands A banded motif moves from an outer edge to a center point and then reverses to the other outer edge. These bands can be stacked one above another or used independently (for example, classic yoke sweaters). When people think of Fair Isle patterns, they usually think of banded motifs.

Symmetrical allover contiguous These motifs connect to each other, forming an unbroken pattern with two center turn points: the motif and the sequences turn twice in this type of design. "Allover contiguous" is quite a mouthful, but traditionally the word "allover" means

that the garment simply has patterning all over and refers to banded patterns, too. You can create allover contiguous patterns from isolated motifs or bands.

Asymmetrical These are the wild card patterns! There are two types of asymmetrical designs: repetitive ones and representational ones. Some Celtic swirl designs fall into the first category; ravens and acorns fall into the second. Asymmetrical designs require more value contrast between the pattern and the background.

Combination Of course, you can use a combination of motif types into a single garment, drawing attention to different parts of your garment.

How Do You Choose?

How do you decide which type of motif to use if you don't have a solid picture in your mind? As you made your speed swatches, certain realities probably became obvious. The most important discovery you made was whether you could incorporate all your color families into a single pair of sequences or not.

Multiple color families If you can create a single swatch that includes all the color families you want, you can choose an allover contiguous pattern or a set of banded patterns.

More than 3 color families If you are working with more than three color families, fitting them all into a single pair of sequences might be impossible. In this case a set of banded patterns will allow you to use all the families you need.

Low value contrast If you prefer a low value contrast between pattern and background, you will probably not be able to use figurative motifs. The lower the value contrast the more you are asking the viewer's eye to fill in the muted areas, so a strong geometric motif that can be mentally completed would be a better choice.

Let your yarn talk to you

Swatch, and swatch again until you've found a combination that works. The proof is in the making, as the same inspiration can lead to very different looks. The photos on the right show how the painted bowl inspired a very literal motif and a geometric one; notice that the figurative motif required higher value contrast.

At this stage you won't be able to pin down your motif exactly. You might find that you have to make some changes when you place your colors into the motif.

ONE INSPIRATION TWO WAYS

A painted bowl serves as inspiration—yarns are chosen from the color families I identified.

One speed swatch (or more) is made.

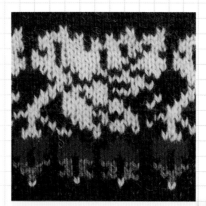

Motif 1. *Figurative.*

Motif 2. *Geometric.*

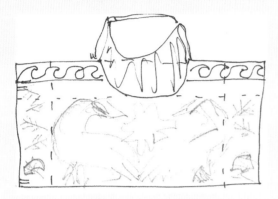

My initial concepts for the sweater were loosely sketched out (above); you can see how it changed by the time I knit the sweater. Little birds flank my initials and the date on one sleeve (bottom).

The Raven Sweater

MY GREAT-GRANDPARENTS immigrated to the Pacific Northwest from Sweden in 1904. They settled alongside the Swinomish Tribal Group in Washington state, and native art forms and stories were a background of my childhood.

I was struck by how traditional Swedish sweaters and Coast Salish tribal art both feature a combination of red and black. I wanted to design a sweater that would evoke both aspects of my personal history without appropriating any particular design element. In Scandinavian style I used only two colors, so this is not a Fair Isle design.

Raven legend The Haida legend of Raven bringing light to humans caught my attention. I sketched out a turtleneck drop-shoulder sweater with simple geometric patterning on the body and sleeves and an asymmetric design on the yoke.

I created the wave, mountain, and pine cone motifs on graph paper. The central sun began as a Scandinavian star motif; I rounded the corners and inserted a raven face in the center, echoing Haida forms.

The geometric Bird Track pattern from *Anatolian Knitting Patterns* by Betsy Harrell is repeated over the body, and the ravens were modified from a chart on Catherine Cartwright-Jones' website. ❖

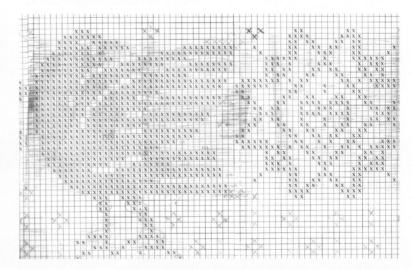

A simple chart made from tables in Microsoft Word, printed out and taped together. I added some motifs and penciled through each round as I finished it.

FINDING MOTIFS

Charts for stranded color knitting can be found everywhere, and you can even make up your own. Thousands of motifs are available in print and on the web. Knitting books aren't the only good sources: look at cross-stitch collections and weaving charts.

Motifs are usually shown as black and white graphs (one student said, "Oh, so that's what those boring black and white books are for!"), although some authors use inscrutable symbols or colors to indicate the pattern.

When you find a motif you like analyze it to see if it is knitable. Are there many very long floats? Can you insert some stitches to break up them up? Can you connect the motifs to make a band or an allover contiguous pattern? Can you isolate part of a pattern to make a small motif?

Planning your motifs offers a real chance to play. Mix and match charts. Move chart elements around. Turn horizontal motifs to vertical ones. Add stitches to make thin lines thick; remove them to make thick lines thin.

Resist the urge to overthink these decisions at the start. Make copies and play around with different arrangements until you are satisfied, but Feral Rule #3 states that you will only know how the motifs will look when you knit them.

Repetition and variation

A successful mix of motifs will include repetition with variation—for example, if you have a band that is 17 rows high, try your other bands at 5 and 10 rows high rather than 15.

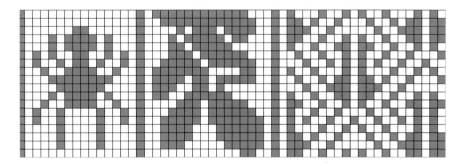

Use contrast

Contrast is important when you are mixing patterns. Large with small, curvy with angular, dark with light. The repetition of these differing elements creates a compelling overall pattern. Vary the visual weight. The human eye looks for symmetry and is enchanted by variation.

MOTIF SURPRISE!

When you are evaluating charts, be sure to anticipate how they look expanded—the space between motifs (known as negative space) creates its own pattern. The little star below creates a set of diminishing boxes as it repeats.

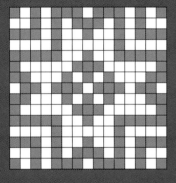

CREATING YOUR OWN MOTIFS

You can let your imagination run free! Doodle with pencil and graph paper until you have created the motif you want.

- Start with a published motif and try adding or deleting stitches, making it larger or smaller.

- Take an isolated motif and turn it into a contiguous pattern by adding connector and filler stitches.

- Examine your inspiration piece to see if it suggests some motifs.

- Look around you. Are there shapes that capture your attention?

 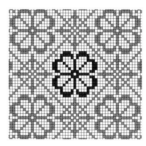 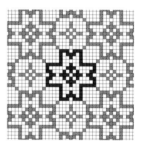

Remember Feral Rule #3

You can't tell whether your motif will work without swatching. Although stranded knitting at a tight gauge can have a nearly squared stitch-to-row ratio, some vertical distortion will occur when you knit the motif, especially if it is an asymmetric representational motif. The heart shape of a knitted stitch doesn't have neat edges.

Furthermore, your decisions about where you place your values affects how the motif appears when knitted—you won't be able to anticipate this until you swatch, so make a decision and start knitting.

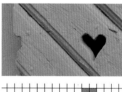

Designing with Bands

Banded designs, perhaps more than any other type of design, are affected by the colors and how they are arranged. It can be difficult to imagine how a seemingly dull banded motif can become a mysterious interplay of patterns! The trick to an interesting banded design is to create contrasts: different pattern heights, visual weights of motifs, and possibly geometric versus rounded forms.

Traditionally there are three types of bands:

Peerie The smallest band; generally 3 to 7 rounds high.

Border: The in-between patterns; 9 to 13 rounds high

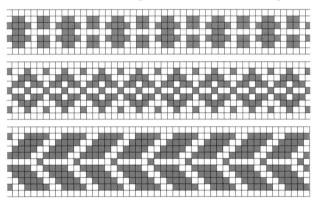

OXO: The tallest bands often consist of lozenge forms separated by Xs—that's why they are known as OXOs.

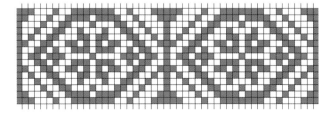

The Redbud Vest

I fell in love with a photograph of flowering redbud branches. But no matter how hard I tried I couldn't fit the colors that I needed—orangey browns, grays, blue-reds, and greens—into a single pair of sequences. Because I couldn't make an allover contiguous design true to the inspiration I decided to make a banded sweater. I designed the wide OXO band first because it is the most complex; then I added the peerie, which frames the border pattern that includes the important touch of green.

Look for banded designs in other cultures: Baltic mitten cuffs, cross-stitch border designs, or African beaded bracelets, for example.

Band-to-band

Interesting things happen where the bands meet: The chart pictured at left leaves a blank area between the patterns where the background of one motif meets the next. This meeting point offers many choices that aren't reflected in the chart—learning to see the possibilities takes some practice. By your choice of value you can create hard or soft divisions between the bands and emphasize band relationships. The Redbud Vest (page 57) shows how the peeries seem to be connected to the border pattern and separate from the OXO; this effect is created by the background values where the bands meet.

Blurring the boundaries

You can blur the band boundaries by creating different patterns where the bands meet. Your background colors can meet as a solid line, of course, but you could also create a jagged edge of knit 1 color A, knit 1 color B, for example, or something even more emphatic—the swatches (below) show two different ways to blur band boundaries.

You can change backgrounds in the middle of a motif. Rather than treating the little peerie pattern in the chart as a band, for example, you could view it as a border between bands, switching background colors at the halfway point. You can also use the same background color for the different bands, letting them flow into each other without a break.

The same three bands are arranged three different ways (above and opposite page).

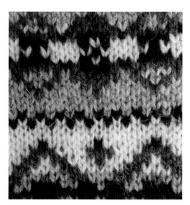

Make a Band Practice Scarf

Understanding how motifs knit up requires real world practice. Treat yourself as you learn with a custom Fair Isle scarf.

1. Find band patterns of different heights, visual weights, and shapes. Print out each one separately. Then cut the printouts apart into separate bands.

2. Arrange and re-arrange the bands in different ways until you find a combination you like. Decide how to treat the spot where the bands meet.

3. Center your motifs in the scarf template (page 146) and fill in your chart, starting with the most complex band (page 64). Or just leap into it without planning!

4. Start knitting. This is a garment to experiment on. When you have knit through your chart once, try again while playing with the colors and adding new bands that may catch your eye. The more, the better.

5. As you continue to add bands ask yourself these questions:

How should the new band mesh with the previous design? Should there be a strong division between the two bands, or one that is very unobtrusive?

Should the band edges have decoration or be plain?

Before you know it, you'll have a new scarf to show off your motif skills.

The Walking Tour Scarf *by Dolly Donhauser shows how exciting bands can be.*

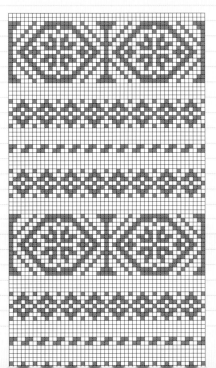
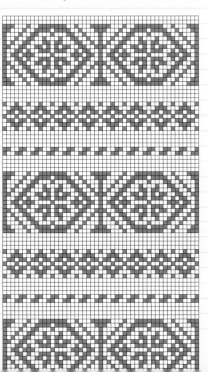

Sea & Sand

THE PHOTOGRAPH OF a Hawaiian beach, replete with golden sand and surfboard, caught my attention. Putting together sequences in the two color families went smoothly, and I quickly settled into the final gradations for an opposing value arrangement.

Motif choice I loved the motif on the cover of *Latvian Mittens* by Lizbeth Upitis. It's a very large motif—49 stitches—but my sequences were long. I envisioned that the golden yellow colors would be in the background and the turquoises to be the pattern.

Swatch surprise
By the time I reached the midpoint of the motif swatch I realized that the value jumps in the golden orange family, which had looked perfect in the speed swatch, were too abrupt when used in wider areas (far left).
   So I switched them: the turquoise, with its smoother value transitions, became the background and the yellow oranges became the pattern (near left).
   Another thing I learned in the first motif swatches was that I wanted a smaller motif, so I altered the pattern considerably.

Design details The pop colors took some work—I returned to the inspiration photo to find the mint and cocoa. The very deep and wide collar needed special attention—I chose a slip-stitch pattern that had the flexibility needed. ❖

Designing with Allover Contiguous Patterns

Although it is more difficult to find the right placement of colors in an allover contiguous motif, garments with these patterns are easy to design: once you find your motif it fills the entire sweater.

Sometimes this can be a little too predictable, so you might want to add contrasting bands or use several allover contiguous patterns in one garment, using a different color story and motifs in the sleeves or the yoke than in the body.

Further interest can be added to a symmetrical allover colorway by breaking the allover motif with a contrasting pattern at the sides, the sleeves, or the yoke.

Starburst Shawl

MEG SWANSEN POSTED a photo of magic lilies that inspired me to try something new: working on a bigger, bolder scale!

Finding a motif After determining the major color families in this photo I made a speed swatch that pleased me (page 40). I remembered seeing some copyright-free motifs charted from old Delft tiles that would be perfect (www.gancedo.edu). They are very large motifs, so a capacious shawl seemed like the perfect flat canvas to work on.

Manipulating the chart I decided on a central star motif and made several copies of the chart. I taped cutouts of the motif in many different arrangements and filled the areas between them with little motifs until I found a knittable composition that worked.

No swatching The final motif was 110 x 110 stitches (about 14" square)—way too large to do a motif swatch. With a bit of trepidation I launched into the shawl without one. It turned out well except that I needed to ratchet up the pop colors. Rather than start again I duplicate-stitched my final choices over the originals until I liked the result. ✧

Shawls offer a chance to play with big motifs and wide bands of color. Because I didn't swatch the motif, knitting at this scale felt risky.

Copies, scissors, pencil, and tape...

Designing with Asymmetrical Patterns

Asymmetrical patterns come in two varieties: repetitive and representational. Actually, you can find repetitive representational asymmetrical patterns as well—trying to categorize motifs is a minefield!

Asymmetrical An asymmetrical pattern can be used in bands or as an allover pattern. The Celtic motif shown below originally appeared as a vertical motif with very long floats. I isolated part of the band, turned it on its side, and added some connecting stitches to make it an allover contiguous design. (Notice that the colors are used asymmetrically, too.)

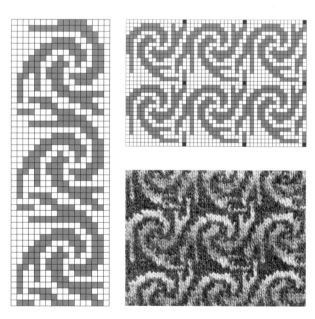

Figurative Figurative patterns offer a chance to let your imagination go wild. Many embroidery books can be mined for figurative motif inspiration. You will have to swatch, of course, to find out whether the motif reads in the knitted fabric.

Opposing value sequences It is very tricky to work with complex opposing value sequences when using asymmetrical patterns. Such arrangements inevitably have an area of close values that obscure the motif; when this is combined with the unpredictability of an asymmetric pattern the motif can easily get lost. Simpler color combinations are better.

Designing Combination Patterns

Feel free to mix and match different types of motifs within a single garment: geometric allover pattern with wide, asymmetrical yoke or bands; geometric bands with asymmetrical bands; a surprise squid in the middle of a symmetrical pattern.

Combination patterns work best when there is significant contrast between the motifs: heavy versus light, geometric versus figurative, sharp versus rounded, small versus large. However, there are no rules except Feral Rule #1: you get to do what you want.

Adding Words

Messages in your knitting, whether inconspicuous or the focus of your design, are a lot of fun and a direct way to tell your story. The letters can be small or large, simple or complex. A simple charted alphabet can be found in *Odds & Ends*.

FILLING IN YOUR COLORS

You've made your motif decisions. Your next step is to put your colors and your motifs together. Filling in charts is most easily done from the center of the motif outward. Keep your yarns lined up in front of you while you work. Remember that traditionally you don't change the pattern color and the background color on the same row (page 11).

Banded Motifs

Here's a step-by-step illustration of how to add colors to a banded motif. This example uses 3 background and 4 pattern colors. Noting the colors on the right of the chart followed by the number of rows knit in that particular color takes you rapidly into the business of swatching. You can tape snips of the colors to your chart if that helps you envision the effects of the colors.

1. Mark the center row (7 in the example). Then working from the center of the motif outwards, begin filling in the pattern or the background (or both). Here I've decided on one row of "Mint" as the pop color in the background. If I hadn't yet decided on a pop color I would just write "Pop" in that row.

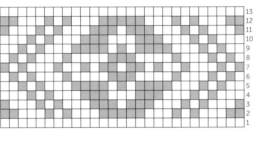

2. Now add a color to the pattern column —in this case 5 rows of Maroon. I could have chosen 3 or 5 or 7 etc; at this stage choosing 5 was somewhat arbitrary.

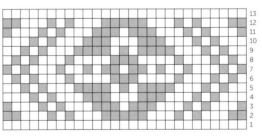

3. Count how many *background rows* sit above and below the center row (6 in this band). Divide theses rows up by the number of colors you plan to use, making sure not to change colors in the same rows as the pattern. I had 6 rows and 3 colors. Notice how the top and bottom color choices mirror each other.

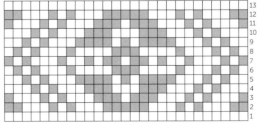

4. Count how many *pattern* rows remain on each side of the center color and divide them up. I had 3 rows and 2 colors. Because I did not want to change pattern colors in the same rows that I changed background colors (page 11), I didn't have many options. Instead I chose to use only one color, Port Wine. I could have changed the arrangement of the background colors if I had felt strongly about using both of my remaining pattern colors. A lot of back and forth takes place while placing colors so be sure to use a pencil.

You can only learn so much from the chart, so when you are roughly satisfied start swatching. The proof of whether your color arrangements will work is in the knitting.

Asymmetric Charts

You can treat these wild card patterns however you want. See if you can identify any natural turning points in your design. Figurative motifs rarely have a natural turning point, so you can mirror your value sequences anywhere that suits your design. Or you can run your gradations unidirectionally—one way, without mirroring. The sole consideration with asymmetric charts is keeping the motif readable, so be ready to simplify your colors if your first swatches are unsatisfactory.

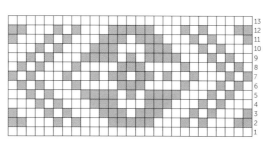
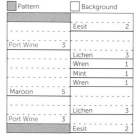

	Pattern		Background	
13				
12			Eesit	2
11				
10	Port Wine	3		
9			Lichen	3
8			Wren	1
7			Mint	1
6			Wren	1
5	Maroon	5		
4				
3			Lichen	3
2	Port Wine	3		
1			Eesit	2

The bottom band was knit with this chart, but the same colors could be arranged in many different ways.

Allover Contiguous Charts

Unlike banded patterns, allover contiguous motifs have two turn points.

Start by marking each turn point and identify colors for each one. Then fill in colors between the turn points. This puzzle is made much easier by having the yarns you plan to use lined up in gradation order in front of you. Play with your yarn—avoid the impulse to intellectualize this process.

Note how the chart shows one and a half repeats of the motif: you need to see both turn points of the design.

1. Mark the two natural turn points—each appears twice. In this example they are rounds 1, 23, 45, and 67. Fill in the pop colors, or write "pop" if you haven't decided yet. In this chart the pop colors have been placed in the background.

2. Fill in the pattern colors at the turning points. These first decisions usually need to be revisited—just look at the yarns in front of you and make a decision. Here I've placed 7 rounds of Olive and 5 rounds of Buttermilk at the turn points in the pattern column.

In this example I'm using 13 colors. They are changing in a fairly regular pattern, but you could divide them up more unevenly. For example, in step 4 you could use 6 Flax, 5 Cashew, 3 Burnt Ochre, 2 Old Gold, which would make the design lighter. You decide which way you want to go by keeping value contrast between the pattern and the background in mind.

When you are fairly satisfied with your chart it's time to knit. Remember Feral Rule #3: you have to swatch to find out if your plan works.

Left chart legend (Pattern | Background):

Row	Pattern	Background
67		Mint 1
64	Olive (7)	
63		China Blue 4
59		Aqua 4
56		Seabright 4
49		Lunar 5
46		Petrol 4
45		Cocoa 1
43	Buttermilk 5	
41		Petrol 4
35		Lunar 5
32		Seabright 4
28		Aqua
24		China Blue 4
23		Mint 1
20	Olive 7	
19		China Blue 4
15		Aqua 4
11		Seabright 4
6		Lunar 5
2		Petrol 4
1	Buttermilk (5)	Cocoa 1

Right chart legend (Pattern | Background):

Row	Pattern	Background
67		Mint 1
64	Olive (7)	
63		China Blue 4
60	Old Gold 4	
59		Aqua 4
56	Burnt Ochre 4	
55		Seabright 4
52	Cashew 4	
50		Lunar 5
48	Flax 4	
46		Petrol 4
45		Cocoa 1
43	Buttermilk 5	
41		Petrol 4
39	Flax 4	
36		Lunar 5
35	Cashew 4	
32		Seabright 4
31	Burnt Ochre 4	
28		Aqua 4
27	Old Gold 4	
24		China Blue 4
23		Mint 1
20	Olive 7	
19		China Blue 4
16	Old Gold 4	
15		Aqua 4
12	Burnt Ochre 4	
11		Seabright 4
8	Cashew 4	
6		Lunar 5
4	Flax 4	
2		Petrol 4
1	Buttermilk (5)	Cocoa 1

3. Count how many background rows remain between the pop colors. In this case there are 21. Count how many colors you want to use: here, 5—4 rows of each color plus 1.

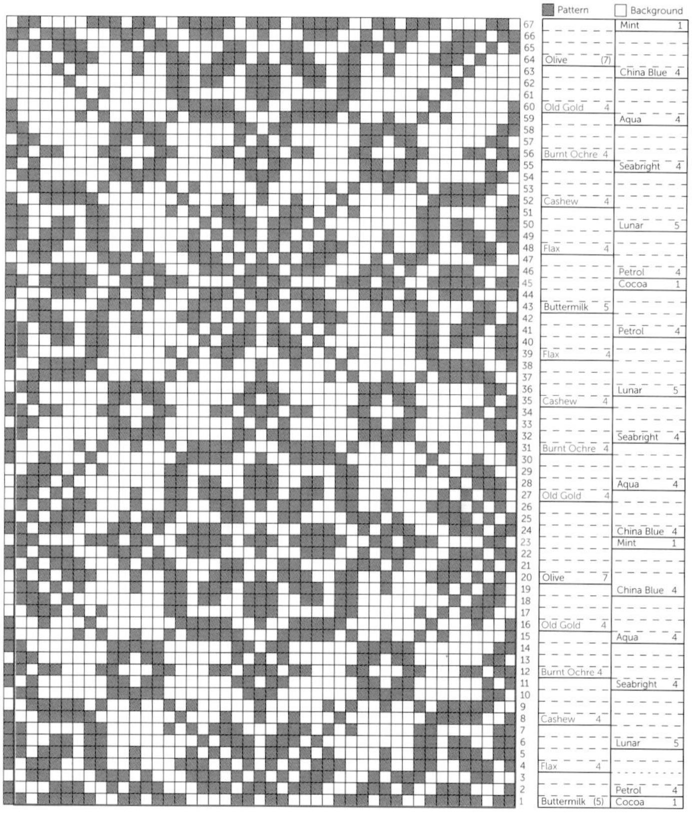

4. Count the remaining pattern rows: 16. Count the colors you want to use: 4. Check to see if there is any conflict with the background color changes and fill in your colors.

Pop Colors

About time! You've been chomping at the bit to choose these fun and exciting garnishes. It's tempting to grab your pop colors at the start of the process, but it's better to leave this design decision until you're filling in your charts.

Pop colors should really be called focus colors: their job is to draw the eye into the center of the value sequences, to the turn point where the sequence and motif flip and mirror themselves. They can be used in the pattern and/or the background; usually they are used in only one round, but sometimes they are used for three rounds. If you are feeling bold you can put them in the pattern *and* the background.

The optimal pop color depends entirely on the colors and values that surround it and on the number of stitches involved. That's why they weren't discussed in the chapter on colors: Until you have pinned down your motif and you know what colors are surrounding the turn points you can't know what your design needs. As a rule of thumb, the closer your pop color is in value to the rows above and below it the brighter it can be without disrupting the design.

Finding your pop color

A pop color isn't necessarily bright or attention grabbing (although it can be). You want a color that will enliven your design, not disrupt it. Start by looking for something in your color families first. Can you identify a color that might fit the bill?

Your inspiration piece might offer some ideas. In the painting shown on page 34 you can see some blue-green in the background that would make an excellent accent color.

By the way, bright pop colors can be used to good effect on the outer edges of a banded motif as well as in the center.

If you are uncertain When you are unsure which pop color to use don't put anything special at the center row of the motif swatch. In the chart simply write "pop" but knit with the colors of the surrounding rows. When the swatch is done, duplicate stitch different pop color options to find out which one works best in this motif.

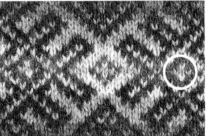

Jamieson Spindrift #180 Mist

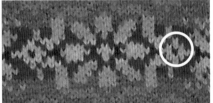

#870 Cocoa

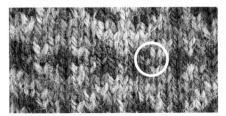

#600 Violet & #1190 Burnt Umber

THE JOY OF COLOR

Recoloring Patterns

Sometimes you find a pattern that you just love—the motifs, the fit, some ineffable something that makes you long to knit it—but you have enough sense to realize that the colors would make you look like you have the flu.

Here are the steps you'd take to change the color story. First it's about value. Then it's about color.

1. Band by band, evaluate the pattern carefully in terms of value and sequencing, Ask yourself: What am I looking at? What types of combinations am I seeing? For example, the large band has a solid color background; the pattern shades from dark to light. The border band has a solid background but the pattern shades from light to dark.

2. Once you understand the values and sequences, take a look at how the colors in the original design work together. How many colors did the designer use? Which color families?

3. Where are pop colors being used? There are two pop colors: the green is used in the background of the OXO and border bands and it outlines the swirly band. The bright yellow pop color appears in the pattern round of the OXO and border bands.

4. At this point you have two options: Either choose your new colors while attempting to match the values of the original or use the original pattern simply as a jumping off point, changing values to suit your own purposes.

The second option gives you much more freedom, and you might be surprised by how different your final garment appears when compared with the original.

5. Now swatch (see Feral Rule #3). Just because you know the patterning works and that you've done a good job of replicating values you can't be assured that the re-colored design will work without testing.

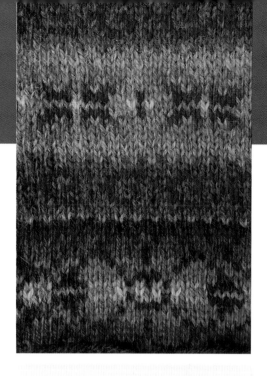

Anne Featonby's Hibiscus Cardigan pattern as it was originally designed (top) and how it looks re-colored (below). Notice that the values in the re-colored version stick closely to those of the original, but the background color in the swirly band is lighter because there was no equivalent value in this color family. The pop colors are used in the same places, and the value sequences are true to the original.

Get the most out of your swatches

✳ Make your swatch as big as you can.

✳ Take a photograph of the swatch—
it's amazing how well a photo can
show what isn't obvious when the
swatch is viewed directly.

✳ Keep good records of what colors
you used in your swatch.

✳ Don't ever destroy a swatch!

✳ Don't make a decision about your
swatch right away—give yourself
time.

✳ Hang the swatch up several feet
away to judge it.

✳ Make a long swatch of unrelated
patterns—no need to bind off/cast
on for each sample.

✳ Use a computer to see how several
repeats of the pattern look—scan the
swatch and then tile the motif in a
page layout application.

✳ Take your swatch outdoors to
evaluate the colors in real light.

✳ Don't forget: the swatch is not
the goal!

Swatching for Color

Now you will begin a series of motif
swatches to find the best combination of motif and color.

1. Start by lining up your colors in
front of you.

2. Fill in your chart.

3. Knit the complete motif—don't
stop halfway, because you really
can't tell if your swatch is successful unless you finish the mirrored
sequences. Don't bind off—it takes
too much time, and small swatches are hard to read when they curl.

4. Analyze your swatch (see *Then
What?*, page 71).

5. Knit a few rows of a different color
and start over until you are happy
with your choices.

Repeat until you find the color and
motif combination you like the best!

If you want to dive in and knit
something other than a swatch, and
you feel pretty certain that your
colors and your motif will work well
together, try knitting a cap, a tam, or
fingerless mitts to test your thesis
before you commit to a full garment.
Templates for these accessories can
be found in *Odds & Ends* at the end
of this book.

Then What? The Self-Doubt Phase

This is the step in the planning process that can derail the most excited knitter—you've been so in love with your idea, and now it seems like dust. What a waste of time and effort!

If you are very lucky your first swatch is exactly what you envisioned. More often than not, however, the first swatches are disappointing. Don't despair, and don't throw out the swatch. Block it and hang it up so you can view it from a distance. Let some time pass. Ask other people what they think. Ask yourself...

...Is there a gap in the sequencing that you find distasteful? The speed swatches are so small that they can hide rough value transitions that show up when the proportions change in the motif swatch.

...Is the overall effect dull? Many yarns are tones, that is, they have a gray undertone that might not show up until you've swatched. Add some clear colors or a complement to perk things up.

...Did the colors brown out? Change the proportions.

...Are all the colors saturated hues? Do you need some heathers? Tweeds? Browns? Tones?

...Does it include colors that were not in the inspiration? It's easy to stray into another color family.

...Or does it lack some colors that are in the inspiration? Figure out what is missing and test it with duplicate stitch.

...Does it miss the emotional feeling of the inspiration? Try changing the proportions of the colors. Make the blue hues dominant, or brighten up the pinks.

...Is the pop color too gaudy? Use duplicate stitch to test other colors.

...Do you need a brighter pop color? Once again, duplicate stitch.

...Does the motif disappear? Visually light motifs, that is, motifs that are only one stitch wide, need higher value contrast against the background than heavier motifs. Opposing value sequences also call for heavier and very symmetrical motifs to work.

Make discoveries, not mistakes! It's not a mistake if you can learn from it. Even the most experienced designers need to make many swatches before they are satisfied.

Your swatches are tools. Set them up so that you can learn as much as possible from each one. If you get discouraged simplify your design—either simplify your sequence relationships or your motifs. Keep swatching until you have created the effect you want.

Forge ahead! In the next chapter you will start planning your garment.

To Do

1 Take a look at your speed swatches. Which ones to you like best? Use your imagination to predict how they will look on a larger scale.

2 Make a decision about what kind of motifs you want to use. Were you able to fit all the color families in your inspiration into a single pair of sequences? If so, an allover contiguous pattern is an option. If you were you unable to fit all the color families into a pair of sequences then a banded pattern lets you put some color families into one band and other color families into a different band. You could also design the body to be an allover contiguous pattern and use the hem, cuffs, and neck bands to add more colors.

3 Plot your colors and swatch. Remember that you can change the proportions—the speed swatch uses the same amount of each color but you can change that in the motif swatches.

Step One Make a chart of your chosen pattern with two columns on the right-hand side. If you are working from a published pattern, tape a piece of paper to the right of the motif and draw your columns there.

Step Two Make several copies of this chart, if possible.

Step Three Sharpen a pencil (trust me—you will regret using a pen!) Fill in your colors, following the guidelines on pages 64–67.

Step Four Using the flat swatch method (page 40), knit at least one full horizontal and vertical repeat of your pattern. If you are working an allover pattern, do at least 1.5 vertical repeats of the pattern. Don't bind off—it's easier to work on a long swatch than small ones.

4 Take a look at the result. What do you think? Use the questions on page 71 to analyze your swatch. Use duplicate stitch to test different pop colors or to smooth value transitions.

5 Knit a few rows in a background color and then knit the pattern again with a new arrangement of colors. Keep knitting a long swatch until you are happy with the result, trying different patterns and colors. You will now understand how your colors work in pattern and be ready to plan the garment.

To Explore

MAKING YOUR OWN MOTIFS

More Sweaters by Tone Takle and Lise Kolstad
The authors walk through the process of creating motifs, from simple dots to complex motifs, with brilliant examples.

Knitsonik: Stranded Colourwork Sourcebook by Felicity Ford
Exciting guide to translating everyday inspirations into knitted motifs.

200 Fair Isle Motifs by Mary Jane Mucklestone.
Visualize how a motif will look colored in or tiled.

Sweaters that Talk Back by Lisa Anne Auerbach
Knitwear as political speech.

MOTIF INSPIRATION

There seems to be no end to the numbers of books that can be mined for motifs! I've listed just a few here. Out-of-print volumes are still be had with some resourceful searching.

Anatolian Knitting Designs by Betsy Harrell (*Turkish*)

Celtic Charted Designs by Co Spinhoven

Charted Peasant Designs by Heinz Edgar Kiewe

Charts for Colour Knitting by Alice Starmore

Colorwork Creations by Susan Anderson-Freed (*woodland animals*)

Complete Book of Traditional Fair Isle Knitting and **Traditional Scandinavian Knitting** by Sheila McGregor

Eesti Labakindad Ilma Laande Laiali/Estonian Mittens All Around the World by Aina Praakli

Enchanted Knitting and **The Tap-Dancing Lizard** by Catherine Cartwright-Jones & Roy Jones (*figurative*)

Latvian Dreams by Joyce Williams

Latvian Mittens by Lizbeth Upitis

Marvelous Mittens by Charlene Schurch (*Komi motifs*)

Répertoire des Frises and **Répertoire des Motifs** by Valérie Lejeune

Selbuvotter: Biography of a Knitting Tradition by Terri Shea

150 Scandinavian Motifs by Mary Jane Mucklestone

To Inspire

How do I define a creative life? Any life that is guided more strongly by curiosity than by fear.
— **ELIZABETH GILBERT**

Go and make interesting mistakes, make amazing mistakes, make glorious and fantastic mistakes. Break rules. Leave the world more interesting for your being here. Make. Good. Art. — **NEIL GAIMAN**

Ideas are like rabbits. You get a couple and learn how to handle them, and pretty soon you have a dozen.
— **JOHN STEINBECK**

To create a world beyond fashion is to summon an emotion or a cherished memory. — **RALPH LAUREN**

Long live the beauty that comes down and through and onto all of us. — **LAURIE ANDERSON**

Everybody can make up their own rules they just don't know they can. ...what's personal is always what's best. — **JULIAN SCHNABEL**

CREATURES OF FAIR ISLE

I was drawn to Princess Hyacinth (Princezna Hyacinta), a painting by Alphonse M. Mucha. I love the colors, the warmth of it, and the way the eye is drawn to the poppy colored flowers in the princess's crown.

I planned to make a cozy, fun, unique cardigan with a critter theme. According to my notes, I wanted "an allover pattern with accent border at cuffs and edges, maybe a slightly different theme at the yoke."

Changes My vision began to change even before I swatched! I found another note to myself, "Be careful! Complex motif plus colorwork may be too much—may lose the motif." Then I started looking for more simplified allover patterns.

My first speed swatch revealed that my initial color selections had value jumps that were too large. I realized that some value ranges didn't work in the swatch even though they were true to the inspiration. The second swatch was more successful.

Search for motifs Finding and adapting motifs to each respective segment of the garment were my biggest challenge. My goal was to have all my motifs meet at the front center (steek) so that when finished and zipped, there would be no break in the pattern. I found my motifs on the internet, mostly on Ravelry. I'd always admired the fish and octopus motifs and paid to download those patterns. Others were free or I sketched them out myself. I

My advice? Don't take your inspiration too literally, or you'll get paralyzed. Allow yourself the freedom to shift the colors, values, families as it seems natural. That is, don't force the colors just because that's what's in your inspiration.

did my charts in Microsoft Excel. I created a grid and then put an "x" in the box to represent the motif. It took a long time to set up, but I could number the rows, change the scale so I could see it better and get a good idea of how the repeats would come together. I also used Janine's row-by-row color assignment technique, designating the background and motif color for each row. This is so much easier than trying to assign different symbols for each color or getting out the box of colored pencils!

The design was never really set in stone. I started the sweater without any clue what I'd do with the sleeves. I also intended to knit it top-down, but couldn't find the right yoke motif and got frustrated. Rather than give up, I started knitting bottom up.

Flexibility Once I got past the corrugated rib, my anxiety about color choices and motifs and design melted away as the pleasure of the knitting took over. Although the designing was fun, I got too wrapped up in it, worried that the overall design was going to be a disaster. I also got hung up on the "rules" of Fair Isle and color sequencing, obsessed with staying true to the color families and fearful of going a little outside of them. But once I started knitting, it just became fun, and I allowed myself to change my mind as I went along.

Through the process, the sweater sort of became what it wanted to be, telling me what I should do next. I allowed myself to abandon early design ideas and to try new ones. Looking back to my original inspiration, it surprises me sometimes how far from it the finished sweater is.

My second piece of advice? A color card is a great way to start, but there is no substitute for laying strands of yarn next to each other, or swatching. If you have the luxury of a great yarn store in your area that carries yarns for Fair Isle, take the time to play with the balls of yarn. Or, buy a sampling of yarn, an entire run of orange-reds or turquoises, for example. Yes, it gets expensive. If you can afford a full set of yarn, that's the bomb! Otherwise, be patient, because it may be hit and miss if you have to order a ball or two at a time. Point is, it's worth it to get the colors right!

I had so much fun designing and knitting this sweater, I was sorry when it was finished. The whole process, start to finish took about eight months. This is the first piece that I've ever signed! This sweater won Best of Show in the Santa Fe (New Mexico) County Fair and a first place ribbon at the New Mexico State Fair. ❖

Pictured left to right:
Spindrift #760 Caspian
Spindrift #365 Chartreuse
Spindrift #179 Buttermilk
Spindrift #462 Ginger

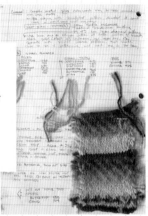

Ginny's speed swatches show parallel value movements, but her complex asymmetrical motifs required her to simplify.

Ginny used a playful mix of figurative patterns, repeating asymmetric patterns, and a mind-bending Escher yoke.

The complex motif emphasizes Lori's feminine design, named for her grandmother. She made many large swatches to get the color placement just how she wanted it.

MYRTLE BEATRICE

I was inspired by Paul Klee's paintings—I have loved his work since I became acquainted with it many years ago, and the colors evoke the era I had in mind so perfectly.

I wanted a romantic, feminine, shaped cardigan with a 1920's/1930's feel. I initially envisioned it in warm gold and ecru tones, with the darker colors used sparingly. My vision remained mostly the same, with the exception of the color palette—that changed pretty drastically as I swatched. I ended up loving deeper values and the contrast between hues—not just dark versus light.

I lifted the main motif out of a Latvian mitten book, after reading Joyce Williams' incredible *Latvian Dreams*. I wanted something curving and complicated and feminine, that could handle lots of colors. I also wanted it to have a very traditional, old-fashioned feel. I ended up drafting the border motif. I'm sure it has also been used by someone somewhere else, but it wasn't in any of my books. I modified something in a Fair Isle motif book until it fit with my vision.

Swatches I knit HUGE swatches! Hahaha!! I had to, to see how all the different colors played together in the large scale motif. I just swatched and swatched, changing colors in and out. I had a hard time letting go of the golds—they just didn't work, but were prominent in my initial vision.

I added "seams" to the sides and raglan sleeves so the pattern change

My advice? Go big!! Try crazy things. You have nothing to lose—it's all a wonderful learning process.

would look better, allowing me to adjust the size and shaping any way I liked without having the increases and decreases look wrong or cobbled together. I used Joyce's mitered, faced edging and button band with grafted button holes. Joyce was pure genius and I'm so glad I got to meet her and show her my sweater. Joyce + Janine = one incredible sweater.

First Fair Isle It was all a big challenge. I had never knit a Fair Isle before, and I hadn't really seen many with the shaped construction and raglan sleeve I envisioned. Most were big drop-shoulder rectangles, which would have done no favors for my figure! I borrowed techniques from so many places, and just sort of winged it, making it up as I went. Learning about color in Janine's class was so empowering. She made it easy to experiment and taught us how to draw a working palette from our favorite images, and then how to refine it until we had what we wanted. Janine took me from ground zero—no experience, crazy-seeming visions, and overwhelming color options—to an amazing piece of art. It's still my favorite sweater after all these years. ❖

Lori pulled yarns from two color families, but the effect is far from simple because she moved from one color family to the other within the value sequences.

Spindrift
#1020
Nighthawk

Spindrift
#794
Eucalyptus

Spindrift
#187
Sunrise

Spindrift
#272
Fog

Nancy's initial speed swatches stuck very closely to her inspiration, an oriental rug.

INSPIRED BY AN ORIENTAL RUG

I was inspired by a very old oriental rug that is in the entrance hall of our home. I love the way natural light affects the colors of the rug as the day and the seasons change, giving it a special depth of color that reminds me of the subtle shading that takes place in a good Fair Isle design.

I began with Janine's speed swatching method, using colors as close as I could to those of the rug. I found that I needed to change directions a couple of times to get the overall effect I was looking for. Once I had settled on my shades of yarn, I played with those colors by motif swatching.

Hunt for motifs My search for motifs was extensive and included color plates from a book of oriental carpets and rugs as well as Celtic and Scandinavian designs. I knew that I wanted a multicolored, stranded garment with only two colors per row. As I looked more closely at the rug motifs, I realized it would have been difficult to express all of the borders and color changes using these parameters. I decided that the garment would have centered, horizontal motifs with vertical panels at the sides to represent the 'border' of the rug. These panels would conveniently continue down the sleeves and absorb the sleeve decreases nicely.

I rejected the initial Scandinavian star motifs because I wasn't getting the strength of colors I wanted. I decided to cast on enough stitches for a hat in order to work through some motifs in a larger scale. I got about half

My advice? Step away from your work often and revisit it after taking a break for a while. Remember to look at your colors and design from a distance. I knew I had the right combination of things when I loved it at all angles!

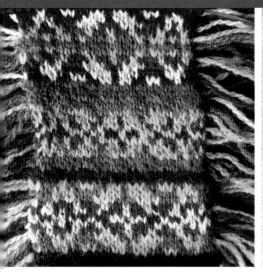

Nancy let the yarn talk to her as her concept went from small Norwegian motifs (left) to larger Komi patterns (right).

way through the hat when I found I really liked some of my motifs (from Alice Starmore's *Charts for Color Knitting*) and wanted to concentrate on them in order to move forward with the sweater.

Sleeve swatch I cast on a sleeve and worked through the cuff design and the first repeats of the best motifs. This 'sleeve' also allowed me to play with how I would do shaping against the side panels. At this point, whenever I questioned my choice of colors, I duplicate stitched an alternate color into the motif to tweak the final design and this was very helpful.

I had to force myself to keep focused on the original design of this sweater and not let my imagination wander to the designs for future sweaters I hope to create! It is tempting to include too many elements into one design and sacrifice the original intent.

Knitting the sweater The actual knitting, once designed, went pretty fast! I designed this sweater to earn my Knitting Guild Association (TKGA) Master title. Since my program required a written pattern with charts to be submitted along with the garment, I benefitted from following my own clear charts and written directions rather than my usual scratchy notes and taped-together copies of charts from various sources.

It helped me to leave my knitting on the back of the couch, walk back into the room, and see it as it would be worn rather than flat on a table. ❖

Pictured left to right:
Spindrift #525 Crimson
Spindrift #301 Salmon
Spindrift #1010 Seabright
Spindrift #1020 Nighthawk

Same colors, very different effects! Feral rule #1: You get to do what you want.

Garment

* Start with the basics

* Add in the details

* Build the pattern

* Estimate the yarn

FROM MANY PARTS TO A WHOLE

YOKED CARDIGAN

VEST WITH RIBBING

SET-IN SLEEVE CARDIGAN

RAGLAN SLEEVE CARDIGAN

You now have a solid sense of the colors and motifs you want to use in your garment. All that remains is to determine the shape of your garment, how the motifs will be placed, and exactly how to construct it.

Thousands of words have been written on how to design garments that fit and flatter; in this book I can only touch the surface. I'm going to focus on the questions that regularly arise in my classes and on the issues that are specific to stranded garments.

Because the construction of accessories such as hats, mitts, and shawls is fairly straightforward, this chapter focusses on garments.

There are so many decisions to make that, once again, you can feel overwhelmed. Ground yourself by referring back to your original planning journal. Answers to the basic questions—who, what, when, where, why—provide solutions to many of the decisions that face a designer. Take it step by step, working from general design concepts to garment details to a detailed pattern, ready to knit.

START WITH THE BASICS

What shape should your garment be?

For many years the only published Fair Isle patterns were boxy, drop-shouldered pullovers and cardigans. This gave stranded sweaters the unfair reputation of being unflattering to all but broad-shouldered men and slender girls. But there is an amazing number of possible garment shapes you can choose from even though you are knitting in the round. Fair Isle knitters have been knitting complex garments for decades; although complex garment shapes aren't hard to plan or knit, graded patterns for complex garments are quite difficult to write so we haven't seen many of them.

Check current knitting publications for ideas about modern garment shapes that you can adapt, but also look further afield—Folkwear sewing patterns, for example, or the racks at your favorite high-fashion store. Search Ravelry and Pinterest to get ideas, checking the project pages to see how the shape you like looks on different figures. If you have a favorite sweater feel free to replicate its shape.

There are very few shapes that cannot be knit in the round! Pay attention to how other designers handle construction details and add notes to your mini journal.

What type of construction?

When you are knitting a garment in the round you are making the fabric and constructing the item at the same time. Learning to think this way can take some time if you are used to knitting in pieces that are seamed together.

Still, when you get right down to it, there are a limited number of ways to construct a sweater: with integral sleeves (the seamless yoke sweater and its variations, such as a raglan); with sleeves added on; or with no sleeves at all.

Any of these variations can be knit from the bottom up, from the top down, or from side to side.

Top down Top down construction allows you to focus on the trickier fit points first, but it can be a little confusing to start with neck and armhole steeks distorting the fabric. It's an especially helpful method for seamless sweaters because the sleeves and the body are naturally at the same point in the pattern and color sequence when they meet. Sadly, the natural advantage of top down construction—that you can try it on for fit adjustments while knitting—doesn't apply when you knit in the round because the steeks make it impossible to try on as you go.

Bottom-up Bottom-up construction is easier to knit because you do not have as much material in your lap at any time; the sleeves can be knit separately and sewn on. You develop familiarity with your pattern and gauge while knitting on the body and can make informed design decisions when you reach the yoke. You also have the option of shaping the shoulders in the round.

Side-to-side Side-to-side construction creates very flattering garments because the horizontal lines inherent in Fair Isle knitting become vertical elements. It's imperative to have an accurate row gauge when plotting a side-to-side garment.

Combination There's nothing to keep you from combining different construction methods in the same garment. Imagine the yoke knit side-to-side, then picking up the edges and knitting the body in the round downwards, for example, or a side-to-side waist band picked up to knit the yoke.

INSPIRATION HUNTING

Fair Isle garment inspiration is only a few clicks away with sites like **Ravelry** and **Pinterest**. Membership is required but free to use these sites.

Garment collections can be found using the search term "fair isle" under Ravelry's Pattern tab. Using the terms "fair isle + sweater + design" will bring up a wide range of pins on Pinterest.

Sewing pattern sites such as **Folkwear. com** are also terrific sources of inspiration, providing useful garment schematics.

Esther & Helsinki

THE ESTHER SWEATER (pictured at left) is based on classic banded Fair Isle yoke sweater designs. I used Elizabeth Zimmermann's Percentage System to make this sweater—I love the fact that there are two unshaped bands a little over 2 inches wide between three rounds of decreases where I can insert patterns.

The simple five-color scheme was inspired by the glorious ceanothus (wild lilac) that grows in California. I chose to use small Scandinavian patterns in homage to my great-aunt Esther. A short swatch of different bands resulted in the final design. I placed partial motifs above the hem and the cuffs—this classic sweater itself has no waist shaping and plain ribbing at the cuffs and hem.

A DIFFERENT APPROACH The Helsinki Sweater is a different kind of yoke sweater. Rather than clustering the yoke decreases in three rounds, I decreased fewer stitches more frequently on a vertical line.

I was inspired by the view of workers at the library across the street from our house: beautiful soft oranges and olives, sparked by the bright orange of the workers' vests. I started with a vertical motif from *Anatolian Charted Designs*, testing the colors in a small cap. I liked it so much I decided that it would make an attractive yoke design. I used Elizabeth Zimmermann's Percentage System to calculate how many stitches I needed to delete from the shoulder to the neck, but I calculated a different decrease rate. I took some graph paper, drew the motif, and then outlined the triangle—I adjusted the motif to fit the shape.

I didn't want to distract from the yoke so the cuffs and hem are simple garter stitch with no patterning. Bracelet length sleeves and waist shaping give the sweater a feminine look. Both sweaters have short row shaping to drop the front neckline for a comfortable fit. ❖

The Esther Sweater uses only five colors and simple bands of Scandinavian motifs.

The Helsinki Sweater spaces the decreases like a funnel—the motif gets smaller toward the neckline.

Explore with a Rough Sketch

Start by making a quick sketch of the garment shape you are considering and then rough in some details such as motif placement, neckline, shoulder line, bands, and pockets. If you don't trust your drawing skills, trace pattern schematics from a knitting magazine or try using figure sketch templates (see *To Explore* for sources).

Placing motifs

When placing motifs you want to be mindful of where you are drawing attention. We notice light areas first, so if you want to draw the eye away from the hips, for example, don't place your lightest colors there.

If you are making a drop-shouldered sweater for someone with a large bust, do not center major motifs; bring them in towards the neck so they don't disappear into the shoulder fold.

If you are knitting for a woman with a larger bust do not give into the temptation to change motifs or run a horizontal band at underarm height—this is very unflattering. Place such elements either above or below the widest part of the chest.

Thinking in color

We can suffer from tunnel vision, thinking of the sweater's body as one unbroken field of motifs. But the body can be broken up into many different areas, with very different motifs and colors. Because Scandinavian designers have excelled at this way of using color and motif I think of this as Scandinavian Color Blocking.

If you want to bring more colors or motifs into your design, think out of the box: place something wildly different up at the shoulders or for the full yoke. Make the sleeves different from the body; the bands wide and unexpected. This is most effective if the areas are quite different from each other: the sleeve motifs rounded when the main motifs are geometric, or small when the main area has large motifs. Contrast is the key word.

Add in the Details

The area around the face receives the most attention. Take care that the neckline is comfortable as well as flattering— you don't want to be tugging at a neck band that wasn't dropped deeply enough. Then design the sleeves and the lower body. Finally, add in the details: pockets, collars, bands, and hems.

Upper Body

Back of neck shaping

If you have ever looked closely at people's heads and necks from the side, you have noticed that some people's necks rise straight from their shoulders while other people have a significant curve.

If you are knitting for someone with a straight neck you might want to do some back of the neck shaping by setting a steek at the neckline approximately 1-inch below the shoulder line and creating a curve.

For people whose necks curve forward shaping the back of the neck is not necessary or flattering—it emphasizes the width of the back and the curve. Leaving the back of the neck straight and decreasing a few stitches across the back of the neck band help it hug the neck.

Shoulder shaping

Taking into account the natural slope of the shoulder when you are designing a vest or a sweater with attached sleeves makes the sweater hang better on your body. Instructions on how to knit a shaped shoulder in the round can be found in *Techniques*; you might also want to explore the possibilities offered by Elizabeth Zimmermann's set-in sleeve in the round (see *To Explore*).

Bringing shoulder seam to natural shoulder

In addition to shaping the shoulders you can bring the shoulder line close to the natural shoulder point. If you

ALIGNING UNDERARM MOTIF & COLOR

If you want the color movement of your sleeves to match the color movement of your sweater, match the color progression at the underarm.

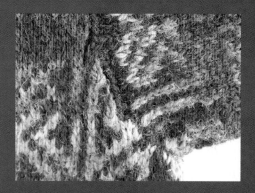

Sleeves can be decreased along the bottom (below) or the top (bottom) of the sleeve alongside a simple seam line or a broad motif.

are planning a drop-shouldered sweater you can inset the sleeve by up to 2" from the side "seam" line without shaping a sleeve cap. This inset can be rounded (see *Techniques* for how to create an easy curve) or squared off.

Armholes

The amount of ease that people find comfortable around the armhole varies significantly. Armhole depth changes with fashion—take a close look at what you find comfortable and flattering. Cardigans, jackets, and sweaters designed to be worn over shirts will need deeper armholes than sweaters meant to be worn on their own.

Vest armholes should be deeper than sweater armholes to leave space for the armbands as well as the clothing worn underneath. When calculating the width of vest shoulders be sure to account for the width of the band—you don't want it sticking out past the shoulder line (known as wings). A useful shortcut for knitting armhole bands that will avoid wings can be found in *Techniques*.

Sleeves and sleeve shaping

Sleeves can be knit from the cuff up or from the shoulder down. When you knit sleeves from the cuff up you don't have the weight of the entire sweater on your needles and the shaping is easier; calculating sleeve length and matching the color progressions at the underarm can be tricky, however. Starting with a provisional cast on above the cuff offers more flexibility—you can lengthen or shorten the cuffs to get the needed total sleeve length.

Knitting from the shoulder down removes the need to match the sleeve width to the armhole opening and you don't have to attach the sleeve to the body. It also takes away the guesswork about matching the color progression at the underarm.

We are used to shaping the sleeve along the bottom "seam" line, but actually you can place your increases or decreases wherever you would like: create a "seam" line along the top of the sleeve, letting the patterns form new designs as you add or remove stitches; run a panel down the top of the sleeve and shape alongside it; run a wide panel along the underside of the sleeve and shape either side of it.

Gussets

Gussets, triangular patches of additional stitches at the underarm, are added to make arm movement possible when wearing very close-fitting sweaters. They are only extra fabric if your sweater has lots of ease.

Lower Body

Length

Your sleeves should not end at the same point as your body because this creates a strong horizontal line at the widest point.

Hems and Ribbing

There are so many ways to treat the bottom edge of your garment it can be hard to choose. Bottom edge treatments need to fulfill two functions: to hold down the bottom edge of the garment, keeping it from flaring out and rolling up, and to frame the garment visually. Cuffs, armbands, neck bands, and cardigan bands finish off the garment and complete the frame, often echoing the colors and motifs of the bottom edge.

Hems Hems are a very stable way to handle the bottom edge of a garment. They also offer a canvas for introducing a different motif.

There are several ways to approach adding a hem facing. Start with the hem, using a regular or a provisional cast-on method, and then purl a round to make the fold—the facing is then tacked down to the body or is knit into the body. Or you can pick up from the cast-on edge to knit the facing. Remember that your stranded row gauge probably differs from your stockinette gauge—to avoid dimpling of the fabric make sure you are on the right round when you connect the facing and the hem.

Hems can be bulky and it is difficult to join the facing to the body without distorting the fabric, so it pays to take

Wait-and-See Edges

When you are unsure about what edge treatments a sweater needs knit the body and sleeves before making a decision. The bands for my Celtic Rose Jacket were not designed until the body was finished and cut open.

When I started the sweater I could not have anticipated the particular shade of green I ended up with. It's fine to wait for an edge inspiration until later in the process.

care when constructing a hem. The hem facing can be knit with a lighter weight of yarn to reduce bulk, or you can reduce the number of stitches by 10%, increasing to the full number of stitches before tacking the hem down.

Ribbing Ribbing in all its forms makes a good, non-curling edge. You can play with color in regular ribbing as in the cuff on page 89.

Knitting the ribbing with a single strand of yarn can make the bands feel insubstantial in comparison to the sweater body. You can double-up the yarn to give the band more heft—and make the knitting go faster. Try holding two different colors together to give added interest.

Garter Garter stitch makes an excellent edging. Holding the yarn doubled while using garter stitch makes the band feel more substantial.

Slip-Stitch Slip-stitch patterns offer the stability of ribbing with more lateral stretch than corrugated ribbing. You can play with using value sequences in a slip-stitch pattern.

Purl-When-You-Can (PWYC) Meg Swansen discovered that you could launch into your motif at the bottom edge of your garment, allowing unbroken patterning without curling or extra bulk by purling when you can.

Let's say that you have a blue background and a white pattern. Decide whether you are going to add purl stitches

SASHIKO

WHEN I MOVED TO the San Francisco Bay area I wanted a sweater that looked a little more sophisticated—I envisioned wearing it with black pants when going into the city. A fitted sweater seemed to fit this vision, so I decided to explore princess seaming coupled with waist shaping and raglan sleeves.

INSPIRED BY WEAVING My first concept involved Scandinavian motifs, but a chance glance at a weaving draft collection revealed the curving motif in the center panel. It seemed somehow Japanese, so I looked at books on sashiko embroidery and researched Indigo boro fabrics and the fishermen's jackets of Awaji Island, where they patch together different embroidered panels.

I chose a classic Japanese sashiko design for the hem and cuffs; the sleeves were inspired by ikat textiles—I liked the idea of contrasting the curving main panel with the geometric sleeves. I made up a nondescript pattern for the side panels to give the effect of a value midway between the sleeves and the center panel. The color story is very simple: four shades of blue against solid white.

COMPLEX SHAPING I used Elizabeth Zimmermann's Percentage System for seamless sweaters to design the raglan sweater. The princess line was made by increasing and decreasing either side of a 2-stitch "seam." I looked at sewing patterns to understand how this shaping works and then laid out the curve on life-size graph paper, but I wasn't sure it was right until I cut open the front steek! The wide front band was an afterthought (page 128). ❖

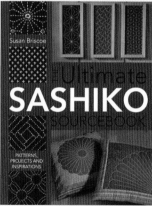

(From left to right) Corrugated rib variation created by using k2, p2 in the background color every third round; classic corrugated rib; k1, p1 rib with gradated color changes; slip stitch pattern with value sequencing; garter cuffs, using two strands of yarn.

to the background or to the pattern. Then, whenever you come to a blue stitch above a blue stitch, purl it—thus purling "when you can."

Start with a single round of k1, p1 rib before beginning the PWYC to tame its tendency to curl; you can also add I-cord if you experience problems.

Corrugated Rib Corrugated ribbing consists of a knit column in one color and a purl column in a second color. Therefore, it isn't a real rib and it doesn't have the stretch of true ribbing; it also lacks ribbing's resistance to curling. To solve this problem start with a round of k1, p1 rib.

If you hold one color in each hand, corrugated rib is a

snap: just hold the purl color in your left hand—it is much easier than bringing the yarn forward from your right hand to purl.

If you want your corrugated rib to glow luminously, use a clear light color in the center and then gradate out using toned colors. You can also create wonderful effects by visually breaking the standard corrugated rib columns.

Bands Armbands, neck bands, cuffs, and front bands are usually (but not always) narrower than the bottom bands. You can use the same type of band as you did for the bottom edge or you can do something different.

For information on how to add bands see *Techniques*.

(From left to right) Classic hem: the hem facing was knit by picking up the cast-on edge and then hem and facing were knit together; purl-when-you-can hem; I-cord edging around a neckline.

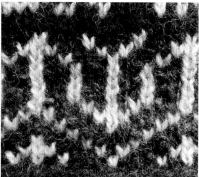
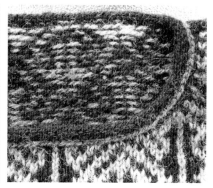

Signing Your Work

What separates a valued heirloom from an outdated garment is provenance: "the history of ownership of a valued object," according to the dictionary.

Perhaps you have seen those touching Swedish sweaters from the 1800s with the owner's initials and date proudly placed on the chest? Or well-worn Selbu mittens with initials and date knit into the cuffs or mitten backs?

Who and when?
Demonstrate the value you put on your efforts by signing and dating your stranded garments. You can place these signs in any hidden spot or set them front and center. Side seams are a natural place, but you can also knit your initials and the date within a motif. If you are knitting for someone else, knit their name into the garment. It's fun to place a longer message in the lining of a hem or a band.

Charting letters It is easy to chart your own letters and numbers with some graph paper. You can also find many complex alphabets by checking cross-stitch motif compendiums. See *Odds & Ends* for a simple version.

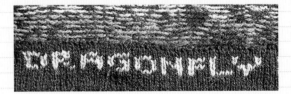

I-cord I-cord makes an effective border for cuffs, necklines, and armholes; you might double or triple it to avoid curling on longer stretches such as cardigan fronts.

Seam Motifs

Traditional Fair Isle designers arrange the motifs to move unbroken all the way around the garment. Breaking the motifs at different points, however, allows us to use large motifs that won't fit around regularly.

Adding seam motifs is extremely flattering—by breaking the main motif and adding a vertical element the visual expanse of the garment at the side is broken. Running a motif up the side of the garment allows you to add waist shaping or create A-line garments by decreasing or increasing alongside the false seam.

This side seam motif can be small (7-9 stitches wide) or it can be a broad panel. The same seam motif can also be used along a raglan line or at the top of a sleeve. These seam motifs can be manipulated to fit the height of the main motifs or they can change independently.

Pockets

You can create horizontal pockets by knitting up to the area where you want the pocket, putting the pocket opening stitches on a holder thread, and casting on the same number of stitches to continue the body. Later you can return to these stitches, remove the temporary yarn, and knit the pocket lining, perhaps with lighter weight yarn.

Do you want vertical or diagonal pockets? Here's where the full magic of steeks comes into play. Vertical pockets are made by placing a stitch on a holder and introducing a steek; bind off the steek when you've reached the wanted height. Diagonal pockets are made the same way, except that you increase on one side of the steek while you decrease on the other side. You can play with the angle by introducing these decrease/increase pairs every round, every other round, or every third or forth round.

Building a Detailed Pattern

You can't make a flattering garment if you don't have accurate measurements. A loving realism is the goal here. Don't fall prey to the "ideal me" measurement syndrome or the "fun house" mirror problem—the first results in garments that are too small and the second in garments that are too large. Neither is satisfactory!

Consult your mini journal

When you began designing your garment you described a general sweater shape in your mini journal. Now's the time to fill in the details. In knitting, every stitch has to go somewhere.

Consider ease

Ease is the difference between your actual circumference and the circumference of the garment. The amount of ease you use is very much a matter of personal comfort; what is considered a fashionable amount of ease changes radically over time so you might as well choose the fit that you will enjoy wearing for years.

The Craft Council of America offers the following guidelines:

● Very close-fitting: Actual measurement or less (negative ease)

● Close-fitting: Add 1-2 inches (2.5-5 cm)

● Standard-fitting: Add 2-4 inches (5-10 cm)

● Loose-fitting: Add 4-6 inches (10-15 cm)

● Oversized fit: Add 6+ inches (15+ cm)

A lightweight sweater, such as one knit out of fingering weight wool, doesn't need much ease to fit comfortably. Try on some sweaters and decide how much ease looks and feels right to you. Cardigans generally require a little more ease than pullovers.

Start with your rough

Using your measurements plus ease and your gauge, you can build a detailed pattern based on your rough drawings:

Pattern Design for Larger Sizes

The distinct horizontal lines of colors in Fair Isle knitting can be problematic when designing for larger sizes, and adding short rows to shape the bust area creates color progression and motif problems. Still, there are a number of ways you can design to flatter larger figures.

In general:

✳ Use narrower value ranges to reduce the horizontal effect.

✳ Use vertical panel motifs rather than horizontal band to break up horizontal lines.

✳ Place large motifs carefully. It is particularly important to avoid creating a line across the bust of women's sweaters.

✳ Knit from side to side, turning the horizontal to vertical.

✳ Design the shoulders first to give a good fit from the top down. Then add stitches for the bust and hips.

✳ Shape the shoulders. Avoid drop shoulder styles, which add too much bulk to the upper body and create a horizontal line halfway down the upper arm.

For larger bust sizes:

✳ Make the front wider than the back.

✳ Use the two-circular-needle method of knitting, putting the front on a larger size needle than the back. This results in a slightly larger gauge over the bust area without refiguring the motifs.

✳ Use extreme shoulder shaping. Extra material built up near the neck can be borrowed to cover the breasts.

For larger hip sizes:

✳ Use a larger needle for the hip area. A minor change in gauge magnifies itself over a large number of stitches to create a larger hip size without altering the motifs.

- Find a similar weight sweater that fits you and take your measurements from it.

- Use Elizabeth Zimmermann's Percentage System as a starting point.

- Go through your books and magazines to find a shape that you like and use those measurements.

- Many books discuss garment design in great detail— please see *To Explore* on page 95.

Plan from the top down

Getting the fit right at the shoulders and bust is key to a flattering garment. After that you can decide how to treat the waist and hips, which in general do not need much tricky shaping.

Some designs require a lot of preplanning; you can just launch into others without resolving all the design issues ahead of time.

On the other hand, you might want to make an even more detailed sketch to scale. This is especially important if you want a certain motif to land at the shoulder line or at the point of a V-neck, for example, or if you want a close fit. This is easy to do when you are armed with your row gauge—basically, you will design up and down from the important placement point.

You can find large sheets of paper or lining fabric that are marked with 1-inch squares. Draw an outline of your sweater and calculate armhole shaping, pocket placement, shoulder slope, and specific motif placement on this type of surface.

Make a custom sloper

If you are planning something with very complex shaping you might want to make a sloper—a sample sewn from heavy t-shirt fabric—to check the fit. You can draw princess lines or pocket placement or necklines onto the sloper and then move these to your pattern.

Place the motifs

Now comes the time to get more specific about placing your motifs. Take note of how tall each motif is. Think vertically: Where do you want the most striking motifs to fall? Do you want a V-neck to start in the middle of a motif? Do you want the corrugated rib to meld into the stranded design at a certain point? Do you need to avoid drawing attention to certain areas? Is it important to you that the motif centers meet at the shoulder?

When you have determined your motif placement you can then calculate where in the color rotation you will be when the body meets the edge treatments, particularly the hem and cuffs. Will this work with the edge treatment you've planned? Or do you need to recalculate the motif placement, the edge treatment, or the garment length?

Or just jump in!

Does all this make you feel anxious? Just start, and let the motifs fall where they may. Cast on provisionally and make band decisions later if you aren't sure what your garment needs. Know which working style works for you!

Write your pattern

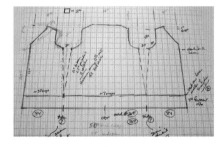

If you've never done this before take a look at how your favorite designer sets up her patterns and use that as a template. Be sure to keep complete records in your mini journal, noting your rationale for every design decision.

As you knit your garment make notes in the journal. It's common to make changes to a design as you go— perhaps you think that you need a different type of sleeve when you see how the body looks, for example.

Center a Motif in 5 Steps

I calculate how to center motifs very visually. There are many more elegant ways to approach this task using formulas, but this is how my mind works:

1 Draw a bird's-eye diagram of the sweater with the total number of stitches. Mark any side motifs you may have decided to use with their stitch counts. If you are planning to make a cardigan you will want to mark the center front in your sketch and add a balancing stitch to make the two front halves equal.

2 Subtract the side seam motifs from the total number of stitches. Divide that number by 2.

3 Now indicate your motif in the center of the front. Note the number of stitches in the motif plus its balancing stitch.

Subtract the number of stitches in the motif (including the balancing stitch) from the number of stitches in the front.

Divide that number by 2. This is the remaining number of stitches on each side of the centered motif.

4 Now, subtract the number of stitches in your motif (without the balancing stitch) from this number as often as you need to get a number that is smaller than that of your motif. That's the important number.

5 Count the number you ended up with in step 4 from the left edge of your motif (without the balancing stitch)—and there's your starting stitch!

You can also use this method to determine the placement of isolated motifs and vertical panels.

Step One

Total Stitches around: 248

Step Two

248 total stitches
- **18** total side seam motif stitches

230 ÷ 2 = **115** stitches front, **115** stitches back

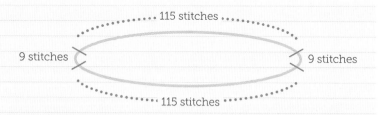

115 stitches

9 stitches   9 stitches

115 stitches

Step Three

115 stitches front/back
- **25** stitches of the center motif + a balancing stitch

90 ÷ **2** = **45** stitches on each side of the motif

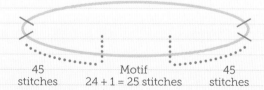

45 stitches   Motif   45 stitches
     24 + 1 = 25 stitches

Step Four

45 stitches on each side of the center motif
- **24** motif stitches

21 stitches

Step Five

The starting stitch is **21 stitches from the left edge** of the motif.

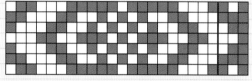

Start here

How Much Yarn Do I Need?

I knew you'd ask that question! It's not easy to answer with any degree of precision because every design uses color in wildly different proportions. Furthermore, floats use less yarn than stitches. There are three ways to approach this calculation:

Swatch for yardage

If you absolutely need to know very specific quantities of each color: make a swatch of a single motif, unravel it, measure the amounts of each color used, and then multiply these by the number of times the motif appears in the garment. Pull out all your hair before you finish!

Rough estimate

If you are OK with generalities, take a look at your planned color use. If your sweater uses 10 or more colors and changes them in the pattern and the background frequently you could start with 2 to 3 balls of each color depending on the size of your garment. Generally the pop color only requires 1 ball of yarn. You will probably have extra balls when you are done, so purchase from a store that will take returns.

Simple calculation

If you want to get fairly specific, try this simple calculation for each color (called Color A):

1. Measure 1 yard of yarn and then count how many stitches you can make at your gauge with this amount of yarn.
2. Add up the number of stitches in one round of the body.
3. Add up how many rounds use Color A.
4. Calculate as follows for Color A: [number of stitches in the round x number of rounds] ÷ # of stitches in 1 yard of yarn = amount of Color A needed for the body.
5. For both sleeves, multiply the result of Step 4 by .33 to find out how much yarn will be used in the sleeves.
6. Calculate corrugated ribs or other two-color bands as you did the body. Solid garment bands need 1-2 balls of the band color; a shawl collar could require 4-5 balls depending on how deep it is.
7. Add the results of steps 4, 5, & 6 to find the amount of yarn you need—a significant fudge factor is built into this calculation as floats consume less yarn than stitches.

Repeat steps 1-7 for each color in your design.

Keep track

If you make a habit of recording how much yarn you started with and how much you ended with for each sweater you make, you will begin to get a good sense of how much yarn sweaters in your size require. In Shetland fingering weight yarn, a tam weighs about 2 ounces and a man's XL sweater weighs 17 ounces, for example.

Dye Lot Variations

Dye lot variations in complex stranded patterns are less important than they are in plain knitting. However, dye lots can vary significantly so it's good practice to have enough yarn on hand to avoid potential problems.

When you can tell that you are running out of a color and can't replace its dye lot, a few strategies can get you out of trouble:

* Start alternating the use of the old and new dye lots rather than using up the old one and then using the new one. If you alternate them it looks like an addition to the pattern rather than a mistake.
* Use the new dye lot in the bands.
* Use the new dye lot in the sleeves, keeping the body in the old dye lot.

To Do

1 Review your initial notes about the project. Has anything changed now that you've settled on colors and motifs?

2 Prepare some rough sketches of your garment.

3 Take your measurements and add ease, or use the measurements of your favorite sweater.

4 Begin to build a detailed pattern with these measurements and your gauge. Calculate where exactly your motifs will be placed. Calculate how the body and sleeves will meet each other. Address construction issues in the neckline, pockets, waist shaping, etc. Or find a published pattern that suits your basic needs and fill in your motifs.

5 Calculate how much yarn you need, place an order, and start!

To Inspire

No project is too ambitious if you crave the result enough. —**ANN SHAYNE**

Nothing, and I mean nothing, is ever exactly as you envision it—ever. Sometimes it is better. —**NATALIE CHANIN**

To Explore

Knitting Workshop, revised edition and **The Opinionated Knitter** by Elizabeth Zimmermann.
Any book by EZ that includes her Percentage System (EPS) is an excellent starting point, whether you are planning a vest, a sweater with sleeves added, or a seamless yoke sweater. EPS has been refined over the years, so use the more recent editions. I also recommend the EZ and Meg Swansen videos, especially Cardigan Details *and* The Fair Isle Vest.

Knit to Flatter (book and Craftsy class) by Amy Herzog.
If you aren't sure what shapes would work best for you, this book offers specific, helpful information about taking measurements, analyzing your figure, and determining the most flattering shapes.

Knitwear Design Workshop by Shirley Paden.
Invaluable and comprehensive design information.

Little Red in the City by Ysolda Teague.
Stellar introduction to fit and shaping of knitted garments focussed on seamless yoke construction with special attention to fitting larger figures.

Yokes by Kate Davies.
Inspirational discussion of yoke sweater styles.

The Knitter's Handy Book of Patterns by Ann Budd.
Templates for sweaters and accessories in any weight of yarn.

http://knittingpatterns.is *Funnel yoke pattern generator.*

Figure sketch templates *Fashionary panels (fashionary.org) and Cashmerette Curvy Sketchbook (cashmerette.com) for larger sizes.*

FAIR ISLE WRAP SWEATER

A picture of an antique tapestry portrait found in *National Geographic* was the inspiration for my sweater. I loved the colors and the muted way they interacted. Interestingly, the color combinations I kept coming up with while swatching were much brighter than the original image. What drew me to such festive choices? My enthusiastic temperament? Or perhaps the gray Northwestern skies?

At the time of the workshop I envisioned a close-fitting, boat-necked pullover to match the shape of my favorite plain sweater. I am always interested in tweaking the boxy traditional shape of Fair Isles.

When Rowan published Marie Wallin's "Izmir" in its Magazine #54, I was really inspired: I'd never seen bands of colorwork on a wrap shape! What a terrific idea! I suddenly knew I wanted to try to apply my design to its shape and translate it for work in the round.

Design details My hardest decision was whether to follow Wallin's lead on her horizontally striped ribbing for the waist and cuffs. I LOVE corrugated ribbing, and hated not to use any, but I couldn't see how to make it work for a shawl collar (and I thought having the waist, cuff, and collar be that different from each other would be distracting). I have in past designs done faced corrugated rib edges, but I worried that to do that here would be too bulky. In the end I think Wallin's solution is, as usual, wonderful. After all, it is a hybrid sweater.

I took the speed swatch with the colors I had chosen at the workshop and began to look for motifs to try. I experimented with different band widths, tried a few peeries to separate them, and varied the relationships of the colors to see what seemed to work best. When I was happy with the results I color copied my swatch,

My advice? Don't be intimidated; just forge ahead and allow yourself to be delighted by the process. Keep experimenting, and let it not be perfect. I see the truth of Janine's advice that ALL swatches will teach you something worthwhile, and if you love color, there will always be joyful surprises.

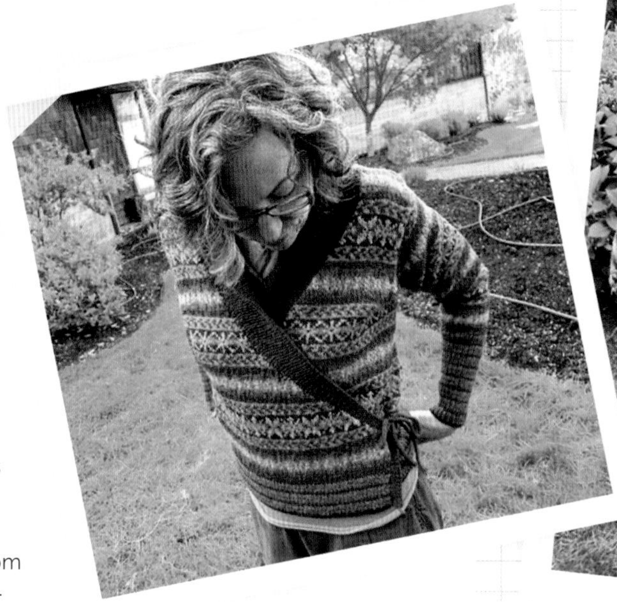

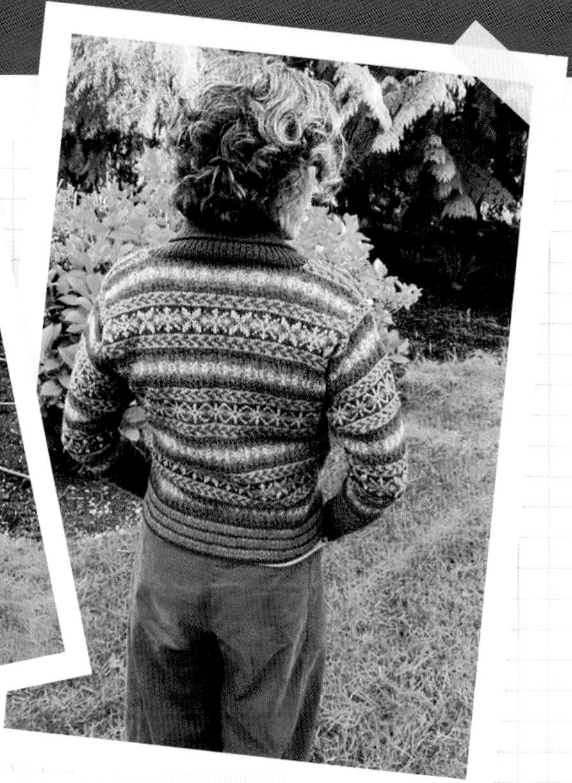

Karen adapted a published pattern, altering it to knit in the round and inserting her own motifs and colors.

cut apart the paper bands, and rearranged them every which way. I then knitted a tubular swatch cap using my favorite combination, for gauge and effect (just binding off the top edges together to make a rectangular hat).

The largest band is from Ron Schweitzer's *Appalachian Portraits*, and the others are out of Mary Jane Mucklestone's indispensable collection *200 Fair Isle Motifs*. I love the way she has made it so easy to find motifs that mathematically coordinate! The math is not my strong suit.

Lessons My biggest challenge only revealed itself at the end of my project: to me, the effect of the colors is not as successful at a distance as up close—and of course I was looking at them from about 2 feet away for months! I tried to get a sense of where things were going by looking at my swatches from far away, but truly the full effect was not apparent until the end. This is a lesson I'm going to have to learn from as I go forward!

Translating the published pattern to an in-the-round construction as I knitted was a question of going step by step and picturing in my mind what needed to happen. I was concerned that it would be hard, but by only worrying about what I was working on at the moment, I kept the task from feeling overwhelming. I kept notes of what I did, in case I wanted to recreate this shape, and it feels like a real accomplishment to have such a new and unusual option in my toolkit. ❖

Karen's use of brown in her sweater adds sophistication to her design—it's easy to overlook the possibilites of murky colors.

Spindrift #526 Spice

Spindrift #825 Olive

Spindrift #766 Sage

Spindrift #425 Mustard

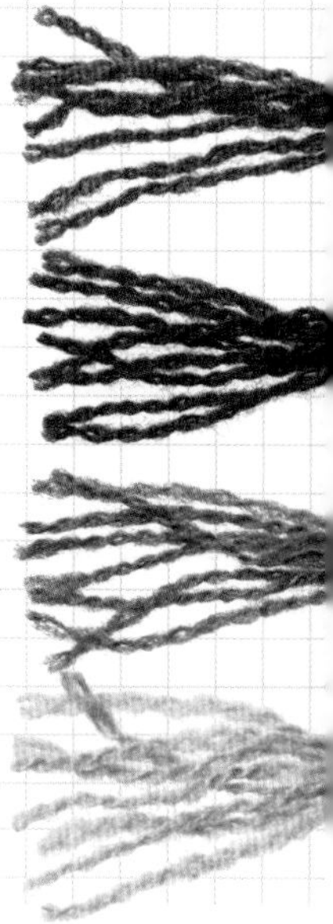

CREATURES OF THE DEEP HOODIE

This sweater was done per commission. My five-year-old son asked repeatedly, over months and in great detail, for a sweater with squid, sharks, octopi, and submarines on it, and then opined upon the designs as I worked on them, which took me about a year.

We had gone to see a show of *ukiyo-e* (Japanese wood-block prints), and I chose the color palette used in Utagawa Hiroshige's Naruto Whirlpool. The background design, both scaly, and to me at least, wavelike in shape was inspired by the curling edges of his famous picture The Great Wave of Kanagawa.

Creating motifs My initial vision was that I'd do a yoke sweater with a repeated fish motif throughout the body, more traditionally Fair Isle in repeat structure.

I drew the motifs using Microsoft Excel. The squid are from scientific drawings (because I didn't really know what they looked like) and all the rest were drawn freehand. When I started swatching, I realized I was drawn to reds that were too dark for the octopi and blues that were too pale for the water. Limiting the color scope was the hardest. I like colors, I want to put them all in.

Evolving design My vision changed as I went through the design process and then through the swatching process. I drew out the whole pattern and colored and re-colored it using Fair Isle color rules for graduations and tone shifts. The hardest part was figuring out what colors made the tone

> *My advice? Don't be afraid to do something you think is hard. The worst that happens is that you don't like it, and you've got a nice pot holder.*

Sarah's decision to use a soft shirt for the sleeves and linings assured that her son would love wearing his special sweater.

shift gradual enough to keep the pattern elements readable. I'm very drawn to shifting colors between warm and cool as well as light and dark, but the design was too complicated for that. I have so many beautiful swatches that I want to go back to and use for other sweater designs!

Figurative motif challenges I did lots of motif swatches to figure out if the patterns were readable. I used duplicate stitch to try out other color combinations.

The hood was a challenge. I figured I'd just wing the hood with the body pattern on it, but figuring out the increases and keeping the hood in pattern as it shaped over the back of the head was hard. However, I steeked it—knit it in the round with a steek and cut it open to make the hood, and I highly recommend doing that for any hood.

Originally I wanted the yoke to mimic the way the ocean gets darker as it gets deeper and go from light at the top to dark, but that required having the motif go from dark to light, and the squid didn't read if they weren't symmetrically colored. Also, it doesn't make sense—giant squid and sharks don't lurk right under the surface of the water, so the whole sweater really is creatures of the deep.

My son is very sensitive to the itch factor, so the hoodie needed a liner, and I didn't want it to be overly heavy because our climate in northern California is so mild. I bought a man's navy shirt from a used clothing store and cut it down to line the sweater, and I sewed it to the inside of the kangaroo pouch pocket to finish that.

The steeks were much easier than I expected! Steeks really aren't hard. Using them makes other knitting easier, like not needing to strand on the purl side, which makes me crazy. ❖

Sarah's colors changed in response to the demands of her complex motifs, which demanded higher contrast.

Spindrift
#168
Clyde Blue

Spindrift
#136
Teviot

Spindrift
#365
Chartreuse

Spindrift
#462
Ginger

Techniques

* Holding the yarn

* Increasing & decreasing

* Savvy steeking

* Adding bands

* Shaped shoulders in the round

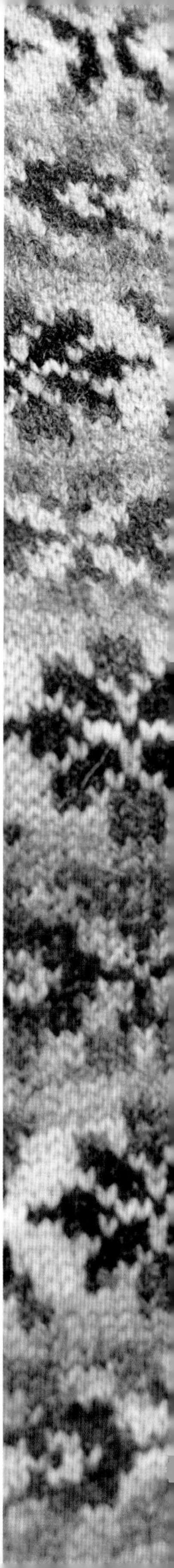

Becoming a Knit Sleuth & Engineer

Shetland Knitting Belts

Fair Isle knitters traditionally hold the yarn in their right hands, supporting their long, double-pointed needles by poking one end into a "makkin belt" — a flattened football of leather stuffed with horsehair and punched with holes to anchor those sharp tips. Use of the belt frees the hands to form the stitches. Usually, but not always, one color at a time is picked up and dropped as needed.

The belt can be awkward at first, but knitting methods that involve a stationary, supported needle are extremely efficient. Scottish knitting teacher and designer Ysolda Teague (pictured above) has a excellent post on her blog about Shetland knitting belts. (Find Ysolda's post at www.ysolda.com/blog/2014/8/21/technique-thursday-knitting-belts.)

Some techniques specific to stranded knitting, particularly questions that regularly arise in workshops or tricks I use, are covered in this chapter. This is not a comprehensive How to Knit section, however. If there is something you want to know that you don't find here—for example, ways to make buttonholes—check out *To Explore* at the end of this chapter. Some subjects are too large and have too many variables to be covered here.

Knitting your own stranded design often requires that you become a sleuth and an engineer, searching out or developing solutions to get the result you want. Purchase books and patterns, studying them closely for construction details—asking if, and how, they could be translated into circular knitting. If your garment requires something you don't know how to do, don't give up. New techniques can be found on knitting forums, in classes, and through dogged historical research.

But if this hard work doesn't seem like fun to you, remember that you can use any published pattern as is, swapping in your motifs and colors for those of the original and taking advantage of construction details that have already been worked out.

Taming the Yarn

It takes time and practice to develop a knitting style that works for you, but it pays off in better fabric and enjoyment.

Holding

Right hand, left hand, or both? There are many ways to hold the yarn when you are knitting with two colors, and every one of them is legitimate if it is getting you the fabric that you want with the least amount of strain on your hands and wrists. If your hands get tired quickly while knitting or if you can't get a good tension, it's worth taking a close look at how you are holding the yarns.

Many people like to knit with one color in each hand, which assures that the yarns don't get tangled.

It is also very efficient to hold both yarns in one hand, the right or the left as preferred. The yarns can be fed off of a single finger or off of the index and the middle fingers. Small tools, such as rings or guides, can be used to feed the yarns evenly; a knitting belt frees one or both hands to form the stitches without having to support the needle.

Once you have found a method that works for you, laugh off any attempt by the knitting police to correct you.

Stitch dominance The stitches coming from one hand position will be ever-so-slightly larger than those from the other position. (This has absolutely nothing to do with which hand you regularly use for non-stranded knitting.) For most people who knit with one color in each hand, the yarn coming from the left hand is the dominant one and should be used consistently for the pattern stitches. If you hold your yarn a different way, check your knitting to find out which position is dominant. The effect of dominance is not always evident while you are knitting—but switching yarn position mid-stream definitely shows in the final project. And there's nothing you can do to alter it after the fact!

Some knitters do not show a dominance effect in their fabric—however, I've never met one. Take the time to find out if dominance plays a role in your knitting (see the sidebar for how to make a dominance swatch).

Stitch dominance is not something you need to fix. You just have to respect it. Sadly, the dominance effect means you can't switch hands depending on whether the background or the pattern has more stitches in any given round to favor your strongest hand position.

GAUGE

"Pay attention" is the unbending rule about gauge! When you design your own garment you don't need to contort yourself to meet someone else's gauge. However, be aware that after you've established your natural gauge, a number of things might cause it to change:

Circumference Many people find that their gauge changes when they are knitting smaller circumferences. If you find this is true for you, just change needle sizes as required to get the gauge you want.

Weight of knitting on the needles It can be hard to establish gauge in the first inch or two of knitting. Once some knitting is hanging off the needles it gets easier to maintain gauge.

MAKE A DOMINANCE SWATCH

To find out whether dominance plays a role in your knitting make a small swatch:

1 Choose two highly contrasting yarns of exactly the same weight. Call one A and the other B. Cast on 40 stitches.

2 Knit 1 A, Knit 1 B. Repeat across. Make a note of how you are holding each color and do not change! So, if A is in your left hand and B is in your right, don't flip them around. If you hold both colors in your left hand and A comes off your index finger and B off your middle finger, don't change!

3 Break your yarn and push your knitting back to the start of the needle.

4 Repeat Steps 2 and 3 until the swatch measures 2.5 inches.

5 Switch how you are holding the yarns.

6 Repeat Steps 2 and 3 until the swatch measures 5 inches. Bind off.

You will probably see a marked difference between the upper and lower sections of this swatch on both the front and back of the swatch.

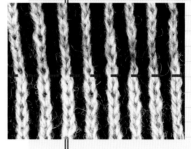

Yarn A (white) held in my right hand: non-dominant.

- - - - - - - -

Yarn A (white) held in my left hand: dominant.

Needle surface Slick surfaces can cause your gauge to loosen, especially if you are a loose knitter. Try using bamboo, wood, or coated aluminum needles.

Needle length Stitches that are bunched up or stretched out on the needle affect gauge. Find needles that don't crowd your knitting or force it to spread out.

Needle size anomalies As if this whole gauge consistency thing weren't hard enough! American size 1 encompasses two metric sizes: 2.25 and 2.5 mm. Similarly, American size 2 encompasses metric sizes 2.75 and 3 mm. Get a needle gauge that measures metric sizes so you can be assured that you are using the same size needles throughout your project.

Diagonal patterns The stitch and row gauges become nearly equal in stranded patterns with strong diagonal lines. You can take advantage of this gauge anomaly by making sleeves or bands that connect perpendicularly look seamless.

Plain vs. stranded People usually have a different gauge in plain knitting than in stranded knitting. For most knitters the stranded sections are tighter than the plain sections, although this is not true for everyone—check your own knitting to find out what is true for you. Don't worry about it—just change needles sizes as needed to make sure the two areas are the same gauge.

The drape of plain stocking stitch differs from the drape of stranded knitting. If your design calls for just a few rows of plain knitting between bands of stranded designs this discrepancy does not create a problem. However, if your design has more than 6 or 7 rounds of plain knitting between motifs, this difference in drape might be a problem. Try stranding your plain areas with two balls of the same color—this gives you the plain area you want while maintaining the fabric's integrity.

Check as you go If you have any concerns about your gauge as you are working on your project, put your knitting on a piece of smooth cotton yarn and block it to make sure you are on track. It's better to know sooner than later, and any subconscious fears you harbor will just hold you back.

Managing Floats

When your floats are the right length you won't have puckering and distorted stitches (floats too short) or excessively long loops (floats too long).

You don't get the right floats by loosening stitch tension! Here's how to get them just right: When changing colors, gently stretch out the knitting on the right-hand needle and hold it in this stretched out position.

Do this lightly; no need for a painful grip on the needle. Now you can tension your new stitch against the last stitch of the same color. When you release your hold, the knitting relaxes into position and the float is the perfect length.

It takes a bit of practice to get this right without thinking. If you are

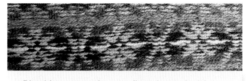
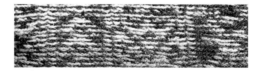

Blocking smooths any float irregularities. Meg Swansen once told me, "If your floats are too neat they are too short!"

struggling, make sure that your needle isn't too slick—knitting that slides very easily on the needle can make it hard to tension the knitting when changing colors. And avoid having a needle that is too short—stitches that are crowded onto the needle try to jump off the tips, creating tensioning problems and difficulties making floats the right length.

When you are knitting smaller circumferences on double-pointed needles or using the two-circular-needle method, pay extra attention to the floats at the points where you change needles. Use one of your fingers to snuggle the floats into the corner created at the needle joins while changing colors.

It is a good practice to set up your knitting so that you don't have floats longer than one inch—if your pattern requires longer floats, you will want to trap the float or set up your knitting for invisible stranding.

Fixing problem floats If you are knitting with wool the floats will felt against the fabric after a few washings, so floats that are bit too long aren't a problem. Very long floats can be cut and knotted.

Sadly, floats that are too short cannot be fixed by blocking. If you notice the problem in the middle of a round you can adjust the floats. If the too-short floats are in only a few rounds you could duplicate stitch over them and remove the original stitches. A radical fix for a few short floats is to snip the float and tie in a short piece of yarn.

Long Stretches of a Single Color

Trapping Trapping, weaving, and knitting in are interchangeable terms for the practice of twisting the yarn that is being carried with the yarn that is being knit to hold it up against the back of the fabric. Trapping is recommended when a float is longer than 1 inch. It's also a helpful technique to use on shorter floats when you are knitting gloves or mittens to keep

Changing Colors

There are several ways to handle changing colors—experiment to find the one that works for you.

Spit Splice

Spit splice, also known as the felted splice, is my favorite method for changing colors because the knitted fabric retains its integrity and there is almost no finishing work to be done. (Despite the name, you do not have to spit on your yarn! Water works just as well.)

1. When you are about 3 inches before the color change, break off your yarn so you have 6 inches of yarn.

2. Unply the yarn to 2 inches from the knitting and break off one ply.

3. Unply 4 inches of the new yarn and break off one ply.

4. Lay the two single-plies together.

5. Dampen your palm by licking it or with a sponge and then rub the yarn to lightly felt the plies just enough to hold them together while you knit them. No need to tug at the felted area to test how strong it is! Continue knitting.

A slight barber pole effect occurs when the colors change. In general this is hardly noticeable and falls under the $10 rule.*

Russian Splice

Use this technique when you need a sharp change in colors at a specific point.

1. With color A knit up to the color change point. Use a coilless pin to mark color A at that spot.

2. Unknit color A until you have about 4 inches of yarn between the pin and the knitting. Break off color A about 4 inches past the marked spot.

3. Unply color A to the marked point and break off one ply.

4. Unply 4 inches of color B and break off one ply.

5. Wrap the two colors around each other at the marked point, laying the single ply end against the same color.

6. Dampen your palm and rub the yarn to lightly felt the plies against the yarn. Continue knitting.

If you've calculated correctly the color change will happen exactly where you wanted it to. If it doesn't just move on! The slightly thickened yarn will not adversely affect your knitting.

Set the unplied strands beside each other.

Fold the unplied strands back on themselves.

Then lightly felt the strands together.

Lightly felt the strands together.

＊THE $10 RULE If you're looking that closely you should be trying to stuff $10 in my bra. I use this rule regularly to remind myself that small imperfections are not worth stressing over.

Knotting

When you need to change colors break off color A, leaving a short tail, and start color B, again leaving a short tail. After a few stitches, tug on the tails to neaten the stitches and then knot them together with an overhand knot, snuggling the knot against the fabric. Trim the ends to about 1/2"—the ends will felt against the fabric when you block it. This is a traditional way to change colors—there is no shame in a less-than-neat interior finish!

Weaving In

You can use the trapping/weaving/ knitting in technique as you go, trapping the new color a few inches before the color change, then changing colors and trapping the old color for a few inches before breaking it off. This can be an insecure method of holding the yarn, however, so make sure that you are trapping the color at least six times before breaking off the yarn.

Darning In

You can change colors by simply dropping one color, leaving a long tail, and starting a new one. When you are done knitting tug on these ends to firm up the stitches and then darn the ends in. Although this is a speedy way to handle the color change, it results in a lengthy job of finishing at the end. If color changes are frequent, the area with the darning will become somewhat stiff.

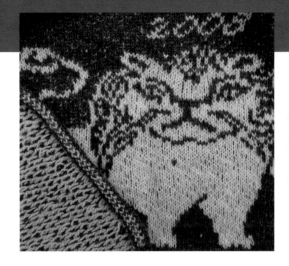

Armenian knitting allows you to place isolated motifs on a solid background; the back of the sweater shows the regular trapping

fingers from catching, and of course garments intended for children benefit from this technique as well.

Trapping is most easily learned by watching someone; many videos can be found on the web. The carried color often peeks through to the front. If you can, trap a color above itself or a color of the same value and be sure to avoid trapping in the same spot on consecutive rows—stagger your trapping points.

Some people prefer to trap whenever a float spans 3 stitches or more. The advantage to regular trapping is that it naturally creates floats that are the right length, and the back of the fabric looks very neat. It also allows you to use motifs that have longer spans of one color. However, trapping subtly changes the gauge and the texture of the knitting, and adds a not-inconsiderable amount of extra movement when you knit. The trapped color usually peeks through the front of the fabric, which can disturb your pattern.

If you are planning a project that utilizes regular trapping be sure to knit a new gauge swatch: regular trapping generally causes gauge to loosen.

Armenian knitting Armenian knitting (so called because Armenian knitters working for Elsa Schiaparelli in the 1930s used this technique, although its origins are not clear) uses regular trapping, even in the plain areas, embracing the color peek through that results from trapping the floats. Regular trapping allows you to make large, isolated motifs while knitting unbroken rounds with two colors, avoiding the use of intarsia.

Invisible stranding This machine knitting technique offers hand knitters an alternative form of trapping that has no color peep through. Essentially it is an interrupted double knitting: in areas where you have large expanses of a single color, add a hidden column of stitches every 3 to 6 stitches and purl into that stitch. (See *To Explore* at the end of this chapter.)

This is what "joining with a twist" looks like after a few rounds.

Casting On

Any cast on you are used to is fine—I use a standard long-tail cast on.

Curling Curling can be a problem if you are planning a corrugated rib, a purl-when-you-can hem, or an i-cord edging. I follow the long-tail cast on with a single round of k1, p1 ribbing. This round is unnoticeable and is enough to stop curling in most cases. If you discover a problem later on add a round of I-cord to halt the curl and provide a decorative element.

Enough yarn If you have concerns about running out of tail before you've completed the cast on, try working with both ends of the ball. Knot the ends together and cast on, then break off the extra yarn when you've finished casting on.

"Join, Being Careful Not to Twist" The injunction to "join, being careful not to twist" is the bane of the Fair Isle knitter's life! When you working with some 200, 300, 400, or more stitches, making sure that they haven't spun around the needle can be tricky indeed.

- Take your time. Straighten out your needle on a table with the working yarn on the right (the right side of the knitting will be facing downwards). Adjust the stitches so they all face the same direction, keeping an eagle eye out for any spot where the cast on has twisted around the needle. Carefully pick up the ends of the needle and bring them together, keeping everything in line. Now start knitting.

- At the end of your first round, do another check for twisting. If you discover that the knitting has twirled around the needle you can twist it into place—but this is your last chance.

- Don't set your knitting down after your first round— knit one more round to be safe.

- You can always plan for a garter or ribbed hem, which you can knit back and forth until you are ready to start the body. Then join, making sure you haven't twisted the hem. It's a simple job to sew up the short seam.

No-Twist Machine Knitters' Trick

Using scrap yarn the same weight as your project, on the same needles as your project cast on the number of stitches you need and knit back and forth until your knitting is about 1 inch long. Then knit a row with a slippery yarn.

Now place a marker and join to start your sweater—it's very easy to see whether that large piece of knitting is twisting around the needle.

When you've knit a few inches, pull out the slippery yarn and bind off the live stitches. (You're right, this is a form of provisional cast on.) This is time consuming, but you can rest assured that you won't have to rip out your knitting and you can save the false hem for future projects.

- Disaster! You've been knitting along only to discover that your knitting is twisted on the needle!

If you have a steek bind off the steek, untwist the knitting, and establish a new steek—no one will be the wiser. When it comes time to cut the steek, the twisted section will straighten out.

If you don't have a steek, you are out of luck—start over, being more alert next time.

Increasing and Decreasing in Pattern

If you are paying attention to your knitting you will be able to increase and decrease in pattern without difficulty. Shading in your chart can help you visualize what is happening. The chart (above, right) illustrates decreasing and increasing on each side of a side seam motif.

Decreasing When decreasing in pattern you want the decreased stitch to hide under the remaining stitch. Remember: the first stitch your needle touches when you are decreasing is the stitch that remains. On the right-hand side of the chart use left-leaning decreases (slip-slip-knit); on the left-hand side use right-leaning decreases (knit 2 together). (Decreases that follow the decrease line, known as full fashioning, distort the pattern and are not recommended.)

Increasing When increasing in pattern pay close attention to the chart. Create your new stitch out of the next natural charted stitch by making a loop; at this gauge an e-wrap works well, but you can use other forms of make one.

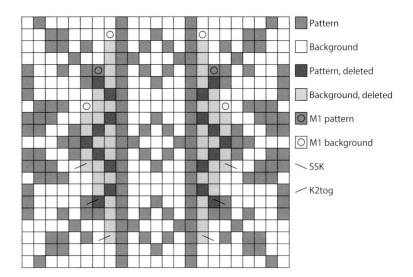

▨	Pattern
☐	Background
▨	Pattern, deleted
▨	Background, deleted
⊙	M1 pattern
◯	M1 background
╲	SSK
╱	K2tog

Karen Hust's marvelous knitted Fair Isle cat is an example of how you can manipulate your knitted fabric radically through increases and decreases. Karen used Sandy Blue's Autumn Tam pattern as a starting point over a fiberglass cat form, with the hat's crown starting the nose.

Steeks

Knitting in the round is a very efficient way to knit stranded patterns because the right side of the work is always visible. However, you need a way to create openings for armholes, necks, and cardigans (and pockets and welted hems and whatever else you can imagine that requires an opening in the knitted fabric).

To do this you add extra stitches where you intend to cut—these stitches are called steeks. The steek stitches don't count when planning a garment; when cut open they fold under to form facings.

If you've never done it before, cutting into your knitting can be a very scary prospect. Don't worry: Every garment I make has steeks in it—and I've never had a steek disaster! With experience you, too, can become casual about cutting your knitting.

Setting up the steek

How you plan to stabilize the steek, how you change colors, and how much of a facing you prefer determine how many stitches you need in your steek.

No matter which method you use, the actual stabilizing and cutting involve only the three center stitches. However, we usually add more stitches to create a margin of safety and a nice facing. The ideal number of stitches you need depends largely upon how you change colors:

- If you use the spit-splice method use an odd number of stitches. I use 7 plus 2 knitting-up stitches.

- If you change colors by knotting or by dropping one color and picking up the other, make your steek wider so that you can stabilize your steek to each side of the loose or knotty stitches. Trim the cut ends once you have cut open the steek.

Set the stitches in the steek up in either **1 x 1 columns** or **speckles** to ensure that the two colors being used are held closely together.

Add 1 stitch on each side of the steek stitches—these are called the knitting-up stitches. Knitting-up stitches function as the base for the bands that are added after the steeks are cut open and are usually knit in the background color.

Important: None of these stitches are counted as part of the garment when you are calculating your pattern.

Stabilizing the steek

There are several ways to prepare the steek before cutting into it. Each has advantages and disadvantages.

The "do nothing" steek When you use a woolen yarn at a tight gauge, you do not need to stabilize the steek before cutting it open. Cut up the center. Trim fuzzy edges. Turn under and use a herringbone stitch to tack it down.
Advantages: Fast. No special equipment needed.
Disadvantages: Takes care to finish neatly. Adds bulk.

The sewing machine steek Using a sewing machine to stabilize the steek is the best solution when you have used a slick yarn or you plan to cut in an area that you haven't prepared for steeking.

Run a line of small stitches up each side of the center stitch of the steek. Stitch another line close beside it. Cut between the lines of stitches (it is easier to see them on the wrong side of the knitting). Fold under and tack down.
Advantages: Very secure. Fast.
Disadvantages: Have to set up the sewing machine. The sewn edges tend to flare.

CROCHETED STEEK STEP-BY-STEP

This is how I prefer to handle steeks when knitting with Shetland jumperweight wool—my method offers secure steeks that form docile, clean-edged facings that require no extra finishing.

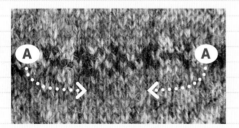

Two outer stitches in background color.

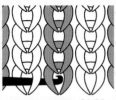

A1 A2   B1 B2   C1 C2

CHAIN STITCH

1. Form a slip knot over the crochet hook.

2. Insert the hook into the knitting.

3. Hook the working yarn and pull the loop through the knitting and through the loop on the hook. Be careful to NOT create a second loop after you pull one through the knitting—that is single crochet and it doesn't work well.

1 Set up the steek My steeks consist of 9 stitches. This count gives me facings that are just the right size. The two outer stitches (the **knitting-up** stitches) are knit in the background color of the garment (**A**). The seven inner stitches are knit in a 1/1 alternating motif/background pattern, either as vertical columns (Figure A) or a checkerboard (Figure B). Note that I change colors by the spit-splice method.

2 Stabilize the steek You will be working on the center three stitches of the steek (identified as stitches **A, B,** and **C** in the diagrams), no matter how wide you choose to make the steek. If you are steeking large areas of plain stockinette, run a basting stitch up the center of the center stitch to help you stay on track.

Using the same yarn you knit the garment with, make a slip knot over a small crochet hook. A 2.5 mm hook works well with fingering weight yarn. Which color should you crochet with? The crochet chain is only noticeable at an unbuttoned cardigan opening, so use any color that makes it easy to see what you are doing.

Chain over a couple of the cast-on stitches before heading up the center of the steek. (See Chain Stitch, right, for crocheted chain stitch instructions.)

Now chain up the steek center, capturing the right leg of stitch A (**A2** in the diagram at left) and the left leg of stitch B (**B1**). Move up row by row, chaining into each pair. Your crochet hook should always move from the outer edge of the steek (where the knitting-up stitch is) towards the center point of the steek, as shown in the drawing. Make the chain stitches firm—the chain should be a bit tighter than the knitted fabric (but don't go overboard and strangle the knitting!). You don't want it to pull a lot, but you also don't want the chain to float loosely on top of the knitting. End by chaining over a couple of the bind-off stitches. Break off the yarn.

Turn your work and chain down the other side, crocheting the left half of stitch C (**C1**) with the right half of stitch B (**B2**).

3 Cut the steek Carefully tease apart the crochet chains to reveal the bars between them. Using small embroidery scissors cut the bars, a few at a time. Don't be in a hurry and don't yank at the edges! Keep steady and try not to cut the crochet chains in the process. If you do, don't panic—you can do a little repair work after the bands are added.

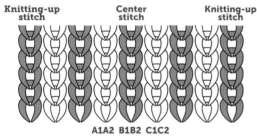

A1A2   B1B2   C1C2

Figure A: *Vertical column setup.*

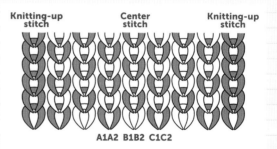

A1A2   B1B2   C1C2

Figure B: *Checkerboard setup.*

Yellow Island

The Yellow Island Sweater, named after a small island in the San Juans, is a play of yellow oranges and blues with a touch of chartreuse. I wanted an outdoorsy sweater with opposing value gradients and an allover motif. The colors fell into place quickly because I was working with only three color families.

I went through several motif swatch cycles but I didn't knit a speed swatch—when you've gained some experience you can skip this step. A dye lot problem forced me to rework the colors, but it turned out to be a blessing in disguise: the final design was better than the original.

DESIGN DETAILS I added a side seam motif that runs up the raglan lines as well, creating its own design as the main pattern decreases on each side—everyone comments on this detail.

I wanted a wide collar and front band, so I chose a knit, purl rib variation. I held two strands of yarn together to give the bands weight, and to add interest I used two different shades of blue, giving a marled effect. ❖

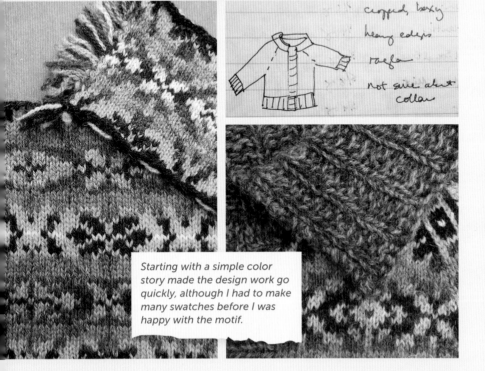

cropped, boxy
heavy edges
raglan
not sure about collar

Starting with a simple color story made the design work go quickly, although I had to make many swatches before I was happy with the motif.

The crocheted steek Crochet a chain stitch up each side of the center of the steek and then cut up the center (page 111). I use this method because I think the neat finish is worth the time it takes.
Advantages: Makes a very neat edge. The crochet causes the facing to lie flat without tacking.
Disadvantages: Slow.

Shaping Around Steeks

Using steeks to create cardigan openings and drop-shoulder armholes is just the start. When you add decreases and increases either side of the steek you can make openings that have angles and curves. V-necks are made by decreasing each side of the steek every second or third round. Angled pocket openings are created when you decrease on one side of the steek and increase on the other every round or every other round. Curves are made by playing with different rates of decrease. Even set-in sleeves can be knit in the round using steeks.

Remember: These increases and decreases are made in pattern (page 109) on the body side of the steek, not in the steek or the knitting-up stitches.

Simple Curve for Crew Necks & Armholes

A nice curve for armholes and crew necks can be created by following this simple calculation:

1. Determine how many stitches you need to decrease.
2. Divide by half.
3. Decrease the first half every round.
4. Decrease the second half every other round.

If you have to decrease a lot of stitches, say for an underarm in an extra-large garment, divide the total number of stitches you need to decrease by three. Decrease the first third every round, the second third every other round, and the last third every third round.

Steek Problem Solving

My crochet pulled out!
Many instructions call for stabilizing a steek by using a single crochet rather than a chain, but this single crochet often fails because it can't be pulled tightly enough, it is bulkier, and it doesn't torque the fabric to make it lie flat. Use the chain stitch! For now, just tack down the steek using a herringbone stitch.

My steek stitches are too loose to crochet!!
This usually happens when people do not use the spit splice method for changing colors, leaving knots or loose areas in the center of the steek. But if all of your stitches are too loose to crochet, then your gauge is too loose altogether. In the first case use the "no preparation" method and next time add extra steek stitches so you can leave a stitch or two between your crochet chains; in the second case stabilize the steeks with lines of machine stitching rather than crochet chains.

My facing doesn't lie flat!!!
This is caused by using single crochet instead of chain stitch or by inserting the crochet hook from the center of the steek towards the knitting-up stitch at the outer edge. Just tack it down and vow to change your ways in the next project.

My steek is unraveling!!!!
This sad outcome is usually the result of trying to steek a slippery yarn, a very loosely knit fabric, or an area that wasn't set up for a steek in which you are cutting through long floats. If you must cut in these circumstances, use a sewing machine to stabilize the knitting first.

Spacing Buttonholes Evenly

So many ways to make buttonholes! The kind of band you are knitting largely determines which one to use. I suggest using a good reference book or an internet search on "knitted buttonholes" to find the one that suits your purposes.

1. Determine the type and size of the buttonholes.

Because knitting stretches and buttonholes get distorted over time, make the buttonholes a tad smaller than the buttons themselves—just large enough to stretch around the button. Multiply the size of your button by the gauge of the band and then round that number down. Make a little swatch to test the size of your buttonhole.

2. Count the number of stitches involved in the buttonhole. For example, if you are making small buttonholes by k2tog, yo, the buttonhole involves 2 stitches.

3. Make a sketch like this example that reflects the number of buttonholes you are making.

4. Count the number of stitches in the band and enter it into your sketch. In the example there are 175 stitches in the band.

5. Fill in the following information (red in the example):
Number of stitches **used in** each buttonhole.
Number of stitches **below the lowest** buttonhole.
Number of stitches **above the highest** buttonhole.

Note: you want fewer stitches above the topmost buttonhole than below the bottommost buttonhole if you plan to add a neck band.

6. Add these numbers and subtract them from the total number of stitches in your band. In the example they add up to 50, so the remainder is 125.

7. Count up the number of spaces between buttonholes (in the example there are 6).

8. Divide the number of stitches in Step 6 by the number you got in Step 7. In the example when you divide 125 by 6 you get 20 plus 5 left over. That means that you will have 20+1 five times and 20 just once. You can see how I handled this by looking at the blue numbers in the example.

9. Add up the red and blue numbers to check that you've calculated correctly! They should equal the total number of stitches in the band.

5 = stitches after buttonhole

5 = stitches in buttonhole

20 = stitches between holes

5 = stitches in buttonhole

20+1 = Stitches between holes

5 = stitches in buttonhole

20+1 = stitches between holes

5 = stitches in buttonhole

20+1 = stitches between holes

5 = stitches in buttonhole

20+1 = stitches between holes

5 = stitches in buttonhole

20+1 = stitches between holes

5 = stitches in buttonhole

10 = stitches before buttonhole

Total stitches in the band = 175

Looking at the band pick-up row from underneath (the steek is on the left).

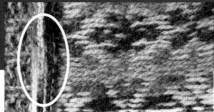

The steek folds over neatly to form a narrow facing.

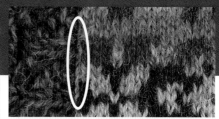

The knitting-up stitch forms a delicate line between the body and the band.

Adding Sleeves & Bands

If you are knitting your sleeve from the shoulder down, pick up the sleeve stitches through the middle of the knitting-up stitches from underneath the fabric. This makes a close and secure join with the body.

Band stitches are also picked up through the middle of the knitting-up stitches from underneath the fabric, which leaves a pleasing line of half-stitches that look like an embroidered embellishment. You want your bands to be attached firmly and to lie flat without pulling in or flaring out. Finding this balance takes some experimentation.

First, be very sure of your gauge. Swatch enough of the band pattern to get an accurate gauge reading. If your initial motif swatch is large enough you can swatch the band right on the motif swatch, which gives you a good idea of how the band would look while you work out the gauge relationships.

Measure these swatches exactly so you can calculate how many band stitches to pick up per rows of body. I pick up in every row of the body and then decrease in the next band row to get the correct ratio; this way there are no gaps where the band meets the body.

Attaching a front band Meg Swansen's method results in a nice join, especially for garter bands. Knit-up row (this is a wrong-side row): Start at the lower left edge of the sweater as you wear it. Using your band needle (usually a size or two smaller than the body needle) and holding the yarn *underneath* the knitting, pull up a stitch through the middle of the knitting-up stitch with the tip of your needle.

Easy corrugated arm bands Here is a no-calculation method for adding arm bands that will not flare:

SET-UP ROUND: Starting at the center of the underarm, with the same size needle that you used to knit the body, knit the live stitches. At the corner where the underarm meets the body, pick up and twist the running stitch to form a new stitch (this tightens a spot that often has a gap). Pick up through every knitting-up stitch around the armhole to the underarm. Once again twist the running stitch between the body and the underarm to make a new stitch. Knit the remaining live stitches and place a marker.

ROUND 1: Using the same needle and the same yarn, [k9, m1] around the armhole. When you are near the end, count the number of stitches you have on the needle and how many remain—fudge a bit to make sure that you will end up with a number of stitches divisible by 4.

ROUND 2 THROUGH THE MID-ROUND OF THE BAND: Work in pattern.

MID-ROUND OF THE BAND ONWARDS: Switch to a needle one size smaller and complete the band.

FINAL ROUND: Decrease 1 stitch at each of the armhole corners and at the top of the shoulder. Bind off.

Crew-neck bands Use the same method to shape crew neck bands. Start at the left shoulder and work around as described in Round 1 (above). Follow directions, decreasing 1 stitch at each shoulder in the final round.

V-neck bands Have you noticed that V-neck sweaters sometimes pull up at the center of the V? The usual ratios of band to body don't apply: the diagonal line demands a 1:1 relationship, if not the addition of an extra band stitch here and there.

Shaped Shoulders in the Round

Classic drop-shoulder sweaters and vests have shoulders that are unshaped—they don't slope to fit the body. They are easy to plan but not very flattering.

Such designs look fantastic on muscular, athletic men and waif-like girls, but have some drawbacks on the rest of us: vests with unshaped shoulders tend to stand away from the body like wings, while in pullovers such shoulders add bulk under the arm and contribute to the problem of the back of the sweater hiking up.

The solution: Use an ever-decreasing spiral—short rows in the round—to create shoulder shaping without having to purl in color pattern.

Knitting the Shaped Shoulder

Materials needed: 4 ~9-inch pieces of cotton yarn, the same size as you've been knitting with; an extra 24-inch or longer circular needle, the same size you've been knitting with, or double-pointed needles; darning needle.

Preparation: Plan your short rows (sidebar). On your final round *before* beginning the shoulder slope cast off the armhole steek stitches.

ROUND 1: Knit in pattern across the front to within X# stitches (calculated in Step 5) of the next shoulder edge.

Put X# stitches on your string, leaving long lengths of string hanging on each end. Then put X# stitches from the back on another string.

Now knit the next available stitch (that is, the next stitch that is not held on the string), which will be a stitch from the garment back. In other words, your active yarn jumps from the front of the garment to the back. Snug this stitch up.

Knit in pattern across the back; when the second color is needed, bring it across from the front, knit it, and snug this stitch up.

Repeat at this process at the other armhole.

You have completed a "short row in the round."

ROUND 2: Because you didn't start Round 1 with X# stitches on a string, you have to fudge a bit now to get yourself set up correctly: Put X# stitches on the string and then put the next X# stitches on the string. Continue around the garment, putting X# stitches before and after the armholes as before.

The floats between front and back have been stretched out (near right) so you can see them; the green string holds the live stitches. The shoulder is closed with a 3-needle bind off to the outside (far right).

ROUNDS 3 THROUGH HOWEVER MANY YOU NEED: Now you are on track to repeat the regular short row in the round until you have reached the height you want.

Very quickly the reduced number of stitches will force you to adopt the two-circular-needle method of knitting a small circumference or else resort to double-pointed needles. Using two circular needles works well because you can keep the back and the front separated logically.

As you spiral around in smaller and smaller circles to the neck, the short rows will seem to baste the shoulders together with sloppy lengths of yarn. That's OK.

Joining the Shoulders

The sloped shoulders are joined together the same way you would join flat shoulders:

Stabilize and cut open the steeks. Put all the active back shoulder stitches onto a needle and do the same with the front shoulder stitches.

Join them using any stable method: 3-Needle Bind Off on the Outside and 3-Needle I-Cord Bind Off are my favorites (see *To Explore* for technical resources).

Any distortion caused by the short rows can be smoothed out later by tugging at the offending stitches from the wrong side.

PLANNING YOUR SHOULDER SLOPE

1. Decide how much rise you want from where your arm meets your shoulder to where your neck rises from your shoulder. A 3/4-inch to 1-1/2–inch rise is standard.

2. Measure the rounds per inch you've been getting.

3. Multiply rounds per inch by the rise you want to determine the number of short rows you need. Add 1 to this number. Example: 1-inch rise = 8 rows + 1 = 9.

4. Count the number of stitches you have allotted for the shoulder— that is, the number of stitches between the armhole steek and the neck steek. Example: 36.

5. Divide the shoulder stitch count in Step 4 by the number of short rows you calculated in Step 3. Example: 36 ÷ 9 = 4. This is the number of stitches to leave behind in each short row and will be referred to as "X#" in the instructions.

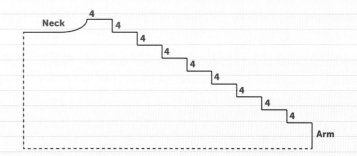

What if you don't end up with an even number? Simple paper-and-pencil math will give you the answer. Let's say you have 41 shoulder stitches. Divide 41 by 9. This tells you that you need to make short rows at 4-stitch intervals, adding an additional 5 stitches somewhere. I like to make rise of the angle sharper closer to the neck, so I put the additional stitches near the arm opening.

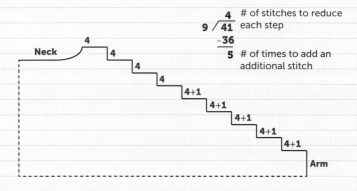

To Do

1 Unhappy with your knitting method? Fabric too loose, floats too short, painful hands? Explore other ways of holding the yarn by knitting an entire cap a new way. It takes time to get comfortable with new muscle movements.

2 Knit a stitch dominance swatch to find out how dominance works in your knitting.

3 If you are afraid to cut your knitting, knit your next motif swatch in the round, adding steek stitches. Cast off, stabilize the steek, and cut.

To Inspire

Without craftsmanship, inspiration is a mere reed blowing in the wind. **—ZOË LONERGAN**

Finding your voice is reaching some sort of balance between the passion to make something and the technical requirements of doing so. **—JOAN COLVIN**

In the crafts, the "time-is-money" attitude is subverted in favor of time-is-care. **—ART ESPENET CARPENTER**

To Explore

STRANDED TECHNIQUES
Knitting with Two Colors by Amy Detjen and Meg Swansen.
This is my go-to source for technical help with all things stranded, including several buttonhole options. Also see Amy's Craftsy classes.

Latvian Dreams by Joyce Williams.
Innovative techniques for impeccable stranded knitting.

Knitting Glossary (video) by Elizabeth Zimmermann and Meg Swansen.
An engaging and easily searched compendium of techniques.

HOLDING THE YARN
Stranded Knitting Techniques: English, Continental...
and In Between (DVD) by Beth Brown-Reinsel.
It is easier to watch someone than to learn from still photos. Beth's informative video includes several methods and trapping information.

FLOATS AND TRAPPING
Trapping is most easily learned by watching videos. Search the web or watch Knitting Glossary or Color Stranded Knitting Techniques.

Armenian Knitting by Meg Swansen and Joyce Williams.
Everything you'd want to know about this art form.

It's Not About the Hat by Susan Rainey.
This comprehensive resource introduces invisible stranding with a 6-page instruction guide, links to 9 YouTube videos, and a hat pattern for practice.

My advice? Don't be afraid to start a patterned swatch if you cannot visualize how the speed swatch will knit up in a finished garment.

BALTIC BOG

From the start I planned to knit a cardigan. My key difficulty was that I could not settle on an inspiration! The initial inspiration—a painting of a pond in indigos, cobalts, golds, and rusts—appeared too bright when I knitted the speed swatch.

I like muted tones with very gradual progressions. I prefer colors to shift in a foggy, almost indistinct progression, so the first inspiration with the brighter colors was problematic. I then turned to two advertisements; both had mossy greens, golds, and muted browns.

Speed swatch frustrations I liked the colors of the second inspirations in the speed swatch, but I was not able to visualize the colors and transitions until I started knitting a motif swatch. The speed swatch frustrated me! I knitted four motif swatches (shown below) before I settled on the final colors.

The motif I chose is common in Slavic and Baltic folk garments. I used the graph for "Sock with Peasant Heel" from *Knitting Marvelous Mittens: Ethnic Designs from Russia* by Charlene Schurch. Designing the sweater's shape turned out to be very easy for me. ❖

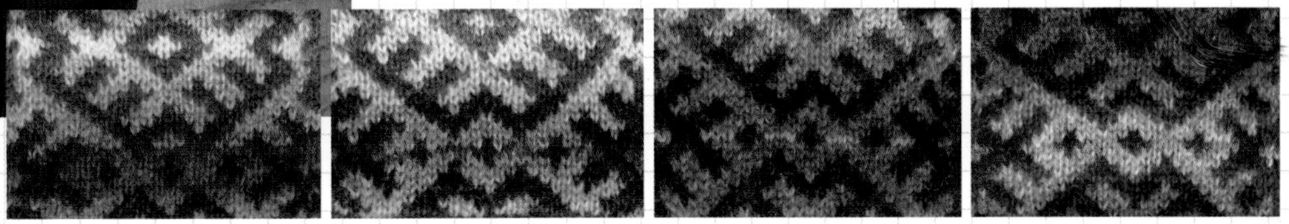

From top
to bottom:

Spindrift
#235 Grouse

Spindrift
#1190 Burnt Umber

Spindrift
#318 Woodgreen

Spindrift
#789 Marjoram

Spindrift
#1130 Lichen

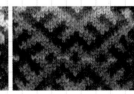

FAIR ISLE SWEATER WITH SET-IN SLEEVES

I chose a photo of a geranium as my inspiration for my sweater: Lots of different shades of red, some white, and many different greens were in it. The reds especially appealed to me.

I began by searching for colors of wool I thought would look good and fit together, and I made a speed swatch for color sequence.

I found the motif in Sheila McGregor's *Traditional Fair Isle Knitting*. After swatching for six different color arrangements I found the one I liked. Since the multiples of the motif did not fit evenly around the body, I used a different 13-stitch pattern at each side (from Meg Swansen's *Knitting*).

Garment shape I started the sweater and the sleeves with provisional cast ons so I could design the hem and cuffs after the body was done. I went down a needle size at the waist to give it a little shaping.

I wanted my sweater to have set-in sleeves. I made my first steeks for the armscyes, then steeks for the neck. I used Janine's shaped shoulders in the round to make the shoulders fit well.

Color challenges My biggest challenges were finding the right colors and then knitting them in the sequence I thought looked best. I used 10

My advice? Take your time deciding the colors in their sequence and keep detailed notes of your progress in a booklet (not in loose pages), including dates and the changes you make while knitting.

Renate tested potential bands by knitting them directly on the motif swatch to see how they would look together.

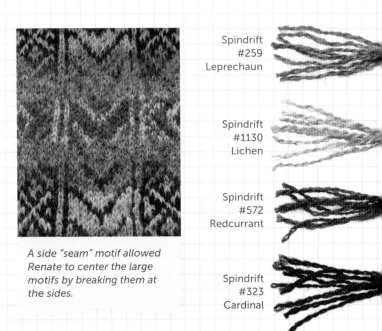

A side "seam" motif allowed Renate to center the large motifs by breaking them at the sides.

Spindrift
#259
Leprechaun

Spindrift
#1130
Lichen

Spindrift
#572
Redcurrant

Spindrift
#323
Cardinal

colors: 6 for the pattern and 4 as background colors. It was labor intensive to take out the provisional cast on (but I would do it again, if I were not sure of how I would like to finish the hem).

Steeking for the first time Crocheting the edges of the steeks and then cutting them was much easier than I expected. Jamieson's Shetland Spindrift is an excellent wool for such a project. ❖

THE JOY OF COLOR

CHAPTER 5: TECHNIQUES **121**

GETTING IT DONE

* MENTAL ROADBLOCKS

* FIXING MAJOR MISTAKES

* FINAL STEPS

"FINISHED" IS BEAUTIFUL!

WHAT DO YOU NEED TO GET A PROJECT DONE?

STRONG VISION of the completed project.

DESIRE to see the project completed.

COMMITMENT to learning the skills to complete the project.

AWARENESS of the mental demons that attempt to derail anything that involves effort—and the development of a loud inner voice to counteract those messages.

SYSTEMS to support the project.

Creating your own original Fair Isle garment is a big undertaking. You start out full of pep and enthusiasm, but somewhere along the line you are likely to notice that the once-loved project is now consigned to the closet floor.

There's no substitute for persistence, a not very exciting quality but an absolutely essential one. Sure, the inspiration is important—the heart, the love, the enthusiasm. The joy.

But inspiration rarely get us through the long hours of creation. Somehow the idea has taken hold that creation is the moment of inspiration, that the follow-through is sort of an after-thought, something to be farmed out to someone else. Less important. The "craft" side of the "art."

Not true. Getting it done is about vision, desire, commitment, self-awareness, and strong support systems. Note that money, time, and innate ability don't appear anywhere on that list!

MENTAL ROADBLOCKS

You might find that you are stalled. The glow of your imagined project has faded, roughed up by the realities of making stitch after stitch. Your mental chatter might be telling you that this is the dumbest design ever, that it won't fit, that it isn't worth finishing.

When you have a quiet moment, pause to figure out what is holding you up. Roadblocks generally fall into a few categories:

Self-doubt

Very often the problem is a lack of self-confidence. "Who am I to think I can design something—don't you need to have Alice Starmore's gifts to do this?" runs your inner chatter. But Alice Starmore wasn't born knowing how to design a Fair Isle; she had to learn, experience failure and success, just as you do.

"If this were a good design I'd want to finish it," goes the committee in your head. But our desires run hot and cold independent of reality.

Honestly, the garment in process is rarely a beautiful thing. Unblocked, it looks rumpled and sad. Without the bands offering design balance and, perhaps, some missing colors, it looks dull.

Pull out your mini journal and re-read all your notes. What was your initial vision for this piece? What steps did you take to get to where you are now? Focus on how far you have come rather than on how far you have to go.

Mental posture is as important as physical posture. Remind yourself that there are millions of quite excellent knitters in the world, but very few people attempt to design their own Fair Isle sweaters. You know everything you need to know to succeed. Of course you can do this!

Perfectionism

The desire for a perfect knitted object often lurks behind those unfinished objects languishing in the corner. Remember that minor patterning mistakes are just the fingerprint of the maker, letting the world know that this object was made by a human being, not a machine. Most of my sweaters have a little error somewhere—even knowing this I have a hard time finding them.

Most errors can't be seen from a foot or two away. Remember the $10 rule when you get obsessed by minor mistakes.

Ponder Feral Rule #2: There is no one right way to do it. The unexamined belief that there is a perfect way to handle these particular colors and motifs often lies behind debilitating perfectionism.

Ask yourself: What is "perfect"? Why do you think that your sweater must be perfect? Keep in mind what's important: you have created your own, unique garment expressive of your vision. A desire to do a good job and pride in excellent construction and fitting skills should not be confused with an obsessive need for everything to fall in line. Worry about a wrong-color stitch is misplaced.

A few seasons ago Ralph Lauren featured a Fair Isle vest with traditional banded motifs. The large OXO at chest level was placed off center—on purpose—to provide design interest and reflect his aesthetic vision. Embrace your imperfection.

WHEN SOMEONE COMPLIMENTS YOUR SWEATER

DON'T SAY

I made a mistake over here.

I intended to do X, but I ended up doing Y.

I think I should have used a different shade of blue in this spot.

The sleeves are a little too long.

DO SAY

Thank you! I designed it myself!

Interruptions

Life throws all sorts of things at us at the most inconvenient times. Large projects are often not well suited for times of chaos, and you might find that you have to shelve your sweater while you prepare for the Christmas holidays, or clean the house for Passover, or plan your parents' 50th wedding anniversary party. And once the sweater is in the closet it can be hard to start up on it again.

Set up your knitting life so that you are able to take your project out of its storage place and begin working on it easily, without worry or mistakes:

● Make sure that your mini journal includes all the critical information for the project: needle size, garment measurements, and yarn color numbers.

● Set up your charts so that you won't inadvertently switch hands when you start the project again, thus avoiding dominance issues.

● Keep all the yarn for the project in the same place— make sure that you've put a note in the bag with the yarn telling you what you're holding it for!

Design uncertainty

You might have stopped because you aren't sure what to do next. You've knit the body, say, but aren't sure how you want to approach the sleeves: Top down? But how to space the decreases? Cuff up? But how to match the colors at the underarm? Before you know it you are stalled for months.

The solution is simple: Action. At a certain point you just have to make a decision and move on. Pull out some

Ducks in a Row

MOST OF US WORK under the assumption that the future will be assured if we can only pin down all the pieces at the start. Get our ducks in a row.

If we can only do that, we think, we won't make mistakes. We will be safe; we will hold chaos and danger and ridicule and censure and shame at bay. So we put all our emotional and physical effort into corralling those unruly ducks.

Comparison In a panic we try to pin things down before we have enough information—a creativity killer for sure. Because we believe that no one else in the world is having trouble getting their ducks in a row, we begin to feel inadequate. We can't move ahead—the consequences of a misstep loom too large. Starting a Fair Isle sweater project by trying to pin down where every color will go in the final design is impossible—until the first swatches are made to see the color interactions, we just don't have enough information to put the final placement in ink. Expecting that we should be able to anticipate how the colors and patterns will work ahead of time makes it very hard to even start knitting.

Letting go The process of designing a complex colorwork garment demands a loosening of grip. Most steps along the way do not produce the results we had hoped for—and it is really, really hard to accept that this is absolutely to be expected. Swatches are intended for learning, not for pinning to a frame and hanging on the wall. Hitting dead ends, starting over with a different concept, throwing the old idea out or turning it on its head—discovery and final mastery comes from a constant stream of mental chatter that says, "What would happen if?" rather than, "I'm afraid that won't work."

Embrace imperfection. Learn from mistakes. Don't judge your insides by other people's outsides. Just start.

Free the ducks!

paper, do some calculations or sketches. Figure out what you need to know to break your paralysis—and then start knitting. Let me remind you: Finished is beautiful.

Over-importance Sometimes we seize up because we've made this project about more than it is. Remember: This is just knitting! Very personal knitting that you are more invested in than, say, a plain pair of socks, but knitting nonetheless. This is about the joy of creation, the fun of self-expression. When you invest the process with too much meaning it can be hard for the reality to live up to the dream.

Your sweater itself will not be life changing—but the process of making it is: stretching your creative muscles, solving construction problems, developing a "can do" attitude, learning to trust yourself.

Having second thoughts Being stalled because of some vague sense that the entire project is a mistake is depressing indeed.

The solution is to try to articulate why the project has become so unsatisfying. Often the discontent is caused by the difference between the initial vision and the knitted reality. A knitting group or an honest knitting buddy can be a real help here by offering objective feedback and constructive criticism.

Sometimes second thoughts arise because you have spent too much time with the project and can no longer see it clearly. Maybe you're even a little bored by it. Perhaps a review of your journal pages will refresh your jaundiced outlook. You might be tempted to set it aside for awhile, but that's a mistake. Keep working, and you will fall in love again.

Maybe your creative mind has moved on to the next design. Don't fight it! Start planning for your new garment while finishing up the one on the needles. Creativity builds on itself—solving the design problems of your current project has probably sparked at least 10 new ideas.

Fixing Major Mistakes

Often we set the project aside because we suspect that something major is wrong with it. The first step is to articulate the problem—you can't fix it if you can't define it. Here's where having a good technical resource or two can help you out, and a cadre of knitters to ask for advice is invaluable.

Here are some common problems:

Too short My Sea & Sand Sweater suffered from this. I don't know why I thought that 12" was enough distance from the cast-on edge to the underarm (I've learned to be more careful when planning my garments—this wasn't the first time winging it had led me astray!). Once I had knit to the shoulders and cut open the steeks I could see that the proportions of the sweater were all wrong. A too-short sweater is easy to fix: run a piece of smooth yarn two rounds above the band, snip a stitch in the round above the band (immediately below the round you secured with the smooth yarn), and unravel that round. Knit up from the band's live stitches however many motifs you need to add the right amount of length, and then graft the sweater back together. You will have to plan ahead to make sure that the color sequences and motifs meet up correctly at the join. When you are fixing an allover contiguous design you will have to graft in two colors—take your time.

Too long Calculate how much length to remove. Snip a round above the ribbing and unravel it to release it. Measure the body and run a line of thin, smooth yarn through the round above the round you plan to cut into. Snip and unravel the round to release the excess fabric. Now graft the ribbing to the new body of the sweater.

Too big You can cut into the sweater, remove fabric, and sew it back together. You could find someone who would fit it perfectly. You could felt it and make pillows or coffee coasters or dog beds.

Too small This is a heart breaker! The second sweater I designed is too small for me. I knew it when I was 4" from the cast on, but I thought, "I'm this far along, I might as well finish."

Well, it is very hard to motivate yourself to finish a sweater that you know won't fit. And when you do finish? You've got a sweater you can't wear.

Solutions depend on how far along you are and how much too small the sweater is:

- If you figure out that the sweater is too small early on, bite the bullet and start over.

- You could try corrective blocking. Remember that blocking wider distorts the row gauge, however, so you might need to add length if it's not too late.

- If you discover the size problem before you get to the underarms you might be able to shift the armholes forward (making the back broader), plan to cut the front open, and add a wide, contrasting panel.

- You could cut up the sides and add extra fabric there.

- You could give the sweater to someone who loves it and will care for it.

Sleeves Not Right The first step is to identify what the problem is. There are three likely problem spots: cuffs, forearms, and upper arms.

Cuffs If your cuffs are too large some hidden rounds of elastic thread can tighten them.

If they are too small, snip a stitch in the round above the cuffs and unravel it. The offending cuff will fall right off.

Now, recalculate your decrease from the sleeve to the cuff and re-knit it.

HAVING 3RD & 4TH & 5TH THOUGHTS...

Sometimes, well, sometimes a project is quite clearly not right.

Maybe you were momentarily enthused by colors that don't flatter your complexion.

Maybe the silhouette you chose because it looks so great on a model just isn't flattering to your body shape, and deep down you know it.

Maybe you realize that you aren't going to lose those extra 40 pounds to fit into the sweater that is on your needles.

In other words, you were in denial when you started out. The sooner you face reality and move on, the better. If you still want the garment, scrap what you've done so far and start over.

If you're done, feeling emotionally detached and ready to move on? It's OK to start something new.

You don't have to finish everything you start. This is not a moral issue! There's no point in using your limited time on Earth knitting something that doesn't give you pleasure.

Toss the unfinished item in the garbage, felt it for pin cushions, or give it to someone who would use it. Put the unused yarn back in your yarn library.

Label your swatches and file them away, knowing that you have learned invaluable lessons—and then use all that freed up mental and physical space to start a new project, smarter and wiser!

Narrow forearms Sometimes, especially when you knit from the shoulder to the cuff, the decreases have happened too rapidly, resulting in a forearm that is too narrow for comfort. Figure out where the right circumference is on the sleeve and rip back to that point.

Upper sleeve woes This can be tricky because changes to the upper arm can affect the join at the armhole. If your armhole is too large you can create a gusset by rapidly decreasing stitches until you have a flattering upper arm width.

Upper sleeves that are too small require major changes, not just to the sleeve but also to the armholes. Can you machine stitch a new armhole opening? The pick up for the sleeves won't be as smooth as if you had prepared for it, but this is minor compared with the effort of ripping back the entire yoke of the sweater.

Major Patterning Mistakes You made a major mistake in the patterning that you just can't talk yourself into ignoring!

If you notice the problem while you are knitting and it's only a few rows down, locate the vertical path above the offending stitch(es) and drop the stitches down to the spot you want to fix. You might need to lay in a new piece of yarn; just knit with it and darn in the ends later. Replacing the dropped stitches can be difficult because of all the floats. Locate the two strands of yarn in the first row you want to restore; capture all the other floats with a safety pin; re-knit your stitches in pattern—repeat until you are back on the round you started on.

If you noticed this mistake long after such a trick would work, duplicate stitch is your friend (although if you didn't notice it until now, perhaps this falls under the $10 Rule—just saying). This is a two-step process:

1. Duplicate stitch the correct color over the incorrect colors.

2. If you leave the underlying knitting in place you can have a texture problem, so snip the wrong color at the center of the problem area from under the duplicate stitch and pull it out. Darn in the ends.

Vaguely not right You've finished the sweater but for some reason you aren't wearing it. This situation is slightly more difficult to figure out. My Sashiko Jacket, for example, fit well and I was pleased with how it looked, but I just never chose to wear it. One day I laid it out on the table and took a hard look. I realized that it needed something to break up the patterning—so I added a wide, seed-stitch band. Now I wear it frequently!

Re-read your mini journal; page through knitting books and magazines. Look at your sweater critically to envision a change that would make you want to wear it. Then do it. You've got nothing to lose!

FINAL STEPS

Caring for your garment will allow you to enjoy your creation for a long time.

Washing & blocking

When you are done knitting give your garment a nice bath to remove all the dust and dirt it picked up while you were working on it. Let the garment soak in a bath of warm water with a blop of pH-neutral dish soap or no-rinse wool wash for 20 minutes, swish it around gently (you don't want to felt it), and support it carefully when you pull it from the water. Add warm water to the wash basin and rinse the sweater as often as needed. Roll the garment in a towel and press out the excess water. If you live in a damp climate you might want to place your sweater in a top-loading washing machine and spin out some of the water or use an extractor.

Stranded knitting can develop a nearly paint-like surface when blocked hard by stretching on a woolly board or by steam blocking (pin your lightly damp or dry knitting to shape and steam it, holding the iron 1 inch above the knitting). Or you can place bath towels on a table and pat your sweater into shape, flipping it over when the top is nearly dry.

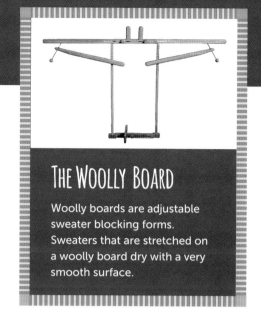

THE WOOLLY BOARD

Woolly boards are adjustable sweater blocking forms. Sweaters that are stretched on a woolly board dry with a very smooth surface.

Storing & repairing

Don't put your unwashed sweater in a dark closet for years. Clean it before storing it and monitor it for signs of moths and other critters.

If you wear your garments regularly you will experience the heartbreak of snags and broken stitches. Take the time to repair these minor problems, and you will enjoy your sweater for decades.

Don't get rid of a sweater that shows signs of wear—learn to darn holes, make elbow patches, re-knit cuffs. Don't use a sewing machine to do these repairs; it will destroy the yarn and create an even larger hole.

You might choose to emphasize these repairs rather than make them invisible. Take pride in these symbols of love and care.

Wearing

Wear your sweater whenever you can—don't save it for special occasions. Let it become your signature in the world, a quiet symbol of intelligence, skill, persistence, and the power of individual beauty in an overly commodified world.

Revel in its warmth, privately thanking the thousands of people who helped you bring your vision to life: the shepherds, the veterinarians, the fence builders, the shearers, the mill workers, the truck drivers, the dyers, the label printers, the shop owners, the teachers, the needle makers, the book publishers, the designers, the editors, your knitting friends—in the deepest sense your sweater is an expression of your place in an interconnected web spanning time and place whose strands are too numerous to name.

Designing your unique, meaningful Fair Isle garment will change how you see the world; colors and shapes will beckon to you as you go about your day.

Don't resist.

To Do

1 If you are stalled, review your original plans in your mini journal. Pull out your work and articulate what the problem is.
   * If it can be fixed, fix it.
   * Commit to working on the project 15 minutes a day until you are done.
   * If it can't be fixed, get rid of it and start over!

2 When you finish, update your mini journal. Even if you don't finish—especially if you don't finish—make notes. There is nothing as demoralizing as making the same mistake over and over again! Weigh the yarn you have left and record the actual amount you used in your garment—this will help you determine how much you need for future sweaters.

3 Share your triumph with your knitting friends, take photos, post on Ravelry, and pat yourself on the back.

4 Neaten your knitting bag, look through your inspiration files, and start something new.

To Explore

Steal Like an Artist by Austin Kleon.
"Go make that stuff!" and other thoughts on being creative.

Wabi-Sabi for Artists, Designers, Poets & Philosophers by Leonard Koren.
Embrace imperfection!

Big Magic by Elizabeth Gilbert.
Your permission slip for living your creative life.

To Inspire

Perfectionism is a refusal to let yourself move ahead. It is a loop—an obsessive, debilitating closed system that causes you to get stuck in the details of what you are writing or painting or making and to lose sight of the whole. **—JULIA CAMERON**

What's the hurry? The satisfaction of one good thing thoroughly made and enjoyed for decades is immeasurable. It's what counts. **—SARAH SWETT**

It may not be easily earned. But when you know in your heart that a cycle can be repeated— not identically, or even nearly in the same way as before—but through a similar process, you own something. What you own is: "I can do this." **—ROBERT GENN**

Spindrift
#580
Cherry

Spindrift
#151
Titanic

Spindrift
#150
Atlantic

Spindrift
#1390
Highland Mist

WOLF OF WINTER STALKING

My inspiration was Jim Branden-burg's photograph of Vermilion Falls (*National Geographic*, June 2003). The photo shows icy cold water rushing over dark grey rocks, with bright red maple leaves framing the shot. The water is mostly white/light grey with a hint of turquoise, the rocks are dark grey with some reddish tinges in spots, and the maple leaves are an orangey red.

The photo has a subdued feel, but the bright maple leaves make it interesting. The caption reads, "September dawns with maples ablaze at Vermilion Falls near Voyageurs National Park. Standing midstream on a rock, I keenly feel the wolf of winter stalking."

My advice? Just jump in and get started! I was a bit intimidated at first when I found myself in a class of some very experienced Fair Isle knitters (I'd only really done stranded mittens and hats up to that point, and only in two colors), but it turns out that not having knit a Fair Isle garment wasn't a prerequisite to being able to figure it out.

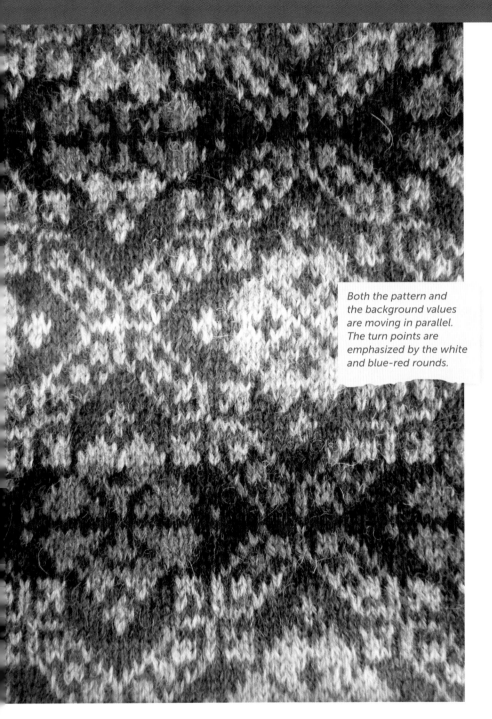

Both the pattern and the background values are moving in parallel. The turn points are emphasized by the white and blue-red rounds.

Initial struggles I planned to knit a cardigan, because that's what I prefer to wear. Other than that, going into the workshop, I had a vague idea that I'd do a traditional Fair Isle design, with OXOs and peerie bands.

When I started my speed swatch, I felt like I just wasn't getting the concept—I didn't like the way my swatch was turning out (of course, I was making this judgment after knitting less than an inch!). I think I was being too literal about using the colors in the photo. There were some very light colors in the water, which is what I started swatching with. I was also trying to use all the gradations of the red, some of which were pretty washed out. But what really drew me to the inspiration photo was the dark granite color and the brightest pop of red, so once I concentrated on the blues and greys and added darker colors, I felt like I had something I could work with.

Pop color indecision I settled on my colors relatively quickly after doing my speed swatch. I had to get over the idea that I needed to use all the colors in the inspiration photo—I just needed to find the colors that gave me the impression of the inspiration and not be so literal. My swatch is mostly blues and greys, with blue-red as the pop color—the first red I used seemed way too bright to me (it's very bright in the skein). So I did a section with some duller reds (the shades of red I might wear in a solid color garment), and it was shocking to me how dull the overall effect was. I really needed that bright pop of color to avoid a muddy look overall.

Motif choices Picking the motif was one of the hardest parts of the process for me. I realized that an OXO/peerie combination would be harder to do for my first Fair Isle garment—I'd picked out lots of motifs that I liked, but I was struggling with how to best combine them, and the color combinations were infinite. To be honest, even though this was the most fun I've ever had swatching, I was impatient to get started—finding one allover design sped up the process (the one I used was from Alice Starmore's *Charts for Colour Knitting*).

Once I picked my motif, I did a relatively small swatch—exactly one repeat wide (again, impatient!). I realized that wasn't going to be enough to really see what the design would look like in a garment—my motif was diamond shaped, so I needed at least two diamonds wide to see the overall effect. It was around the time I started my third, bigger swatch that I really got hooked on swatching just to see how the motifs and colors looked!

I played around a bit with the color transitions. Even using the colors in the same order, shifting the rows in which I changed colors made a big difference; where I had obvious wide stripes (not the effect I was going for), by adjusting the color transitions by just one row I was able to achieve a much more subtle transition.

Swatching Embrace the swatching process! I really did enjoy swatching and didn't mind doing another pattern repeat with a slightly different grey or blue, just to see what effect that would have on the overall appearance.

I never really thought I had much of a sense of color or that I'd be able to figure out which colors to use. I'd read quite a bit on color theory but didn't feel confident putting colors together. Starting with an inspiration piece is just genius—it really helps to have a guide (but also know that you can stray from the guide if it's not working for you). ❖

Karen didn't want to interrupt her large allover contiguous motif, so she chose an inconspicuous edge treatment.

Karen's color story changed as she swatched.

THE JOY OF COLOR

Spindrift
#147 Moss

Spindrift
#787 Jade

Spindrift
#780 Lime

Spindrift
#470 Pumpkin

INTO THE JUNGLE

My collection of inspiration photos were all very similar—I kept being drawn to the same color theme. My initial vision of the garment was very vague; as I continued through the process of swatching with different motifs, the shape of the garment started to take form. At first I wasn't sure if it would be a cardigan or pullover, but I knew it would be for me.

I used Janine's speed swatching techniques with my color choices. From my inspiration picture I was able to find many colors of yarn that were possibilities. During the speed swatching I was able to narrow my choices to a workable number of colors.

Testing motifs Once I found combinations and transitions that created the look that I wanted I moved to working with motifs. At first I tried a motif that involved a higher percentage of background colors but that just did not give me the look I was after. I then tried several motifs that were fairly balanced between the background and foreground and settled upon the ones in the sweater. These motifs came from Alice Starmore's *Charts for Colour Knitting*. I did offset the designs a bit.

Because I didn't know what I wanted to use for the bottom band, I skipped that—I worked a provisional cast on and started directly on the body.

Sleeve experimentation The idea of changing the pattern for the sleeves came after the body was knit while I was thinking of what type of design to use for the bottom band and the front bands/shawl collar. Initially, the sleeves were going to match the body, but after figuring out how the bands would appear, I wanted something that would not be as busy as the body motif.

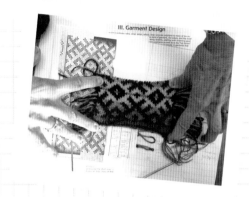

I really liked the idea of having the sleeves consist of a greater percentage of a duller background color and a geometric design, in contrast to the bright colors of the main body design. In theory it sounded like it would balance out the brilliance of the body, but in reality it just did not work. I lost the balance between the colors that is so striking in the body. So I forged ahead using the main body design on the sleeves. I thought I could tone down the brightness of the whole top when I got to the bands.

Collar & bands While working the very geometric motif of the body, the idea of a shawl collar appealed to me, as the softness of the collar would offset the squareness of the body motif. I allowed myself to make decisions as I came to the points where they needed to be made, such as the collar area.

All the while that I was knitting the sleeves I was thinking of how I was going to tie in the shawl collar, cuffs, and bottom band. I knew that the shawl collar would have to be reversible, so corrugated ribbing would not work. When I got to the cuffs I gave double knitting a try. Again I ran into the problem of creating the striking effect of the color changes on a solid background. It just did not play out like my visions.

Eventually the idea of brioche came to mind. Once that popped into my head, I could go full steam ahead with the bands. I kept the same color sequencing in the bands as the body, but in a toned down version, eliminating some of the colors. I used more of the bright yellow green to balance out all of the oranges of the body. Figuring out how to make nice neat buttonholes in the brioche took a little experimenting but worked out nicely.

Persistence There were times I had to stop knitting because I ran into roadblocks with my thinking. Each time I could not be clear about the next design element, I would have to stop. The ideas had to percolate, mostly while I was sleeping, and then suddenly I would have an "aha" moment and the next steps would be clear in my mind.

Initially, my biggest challenge was making sure that the color pattern was balanced on the body without having a large band across the bust area. The next biggest challenge was making the transition from the body to the bottom band work. It took quite a bit of swatching to find the right gauge to transition from the stockinette stitch of the body to the brioche knitting of the bands.

The easiest part was the knitting itself. Once I could envision what I wanted and put that on paper, the knitting went fairly smoothly and quickly. ❖

Knitting the body before designing the bands and collar allowed Suzanne to see clearly what would work best.

Suzanne closed the shaped shoulders with a modified 3-needle bind off.

I believe we should glory in the evidence of
the human maker, glory in the imperfections,
the variations from standard, that make
our work, and us, something you cannot buy,
something precious in this world,
something unique.

— Sara Lamb

Odds & Ends

* Speed swatching chart

* Chart and knit...
  ...a cap
  ...a tam
  ...& more

* Blank planning paper

Speed Swatch Chart

Arrange your colors in two sequences—Sequence A and Sequence B—as described on page 39.

Add the colors to the columns on the right of the chart.

Cast on 20 stitches with the first color in Sequence A.

Follow the chart until you've used all your colors. If you are knitting a really lengthy sequence you might run out of chart—but by then you will have internalized the pattern!

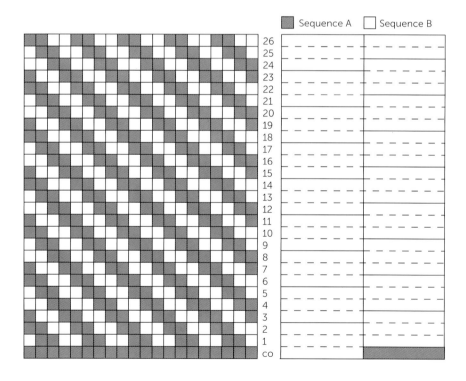

BLANK PLANNING PAPER

Because stranded knitting at a close gauge has a nearly 1:1 stitch:row gauge, I use square graph paper for planning.

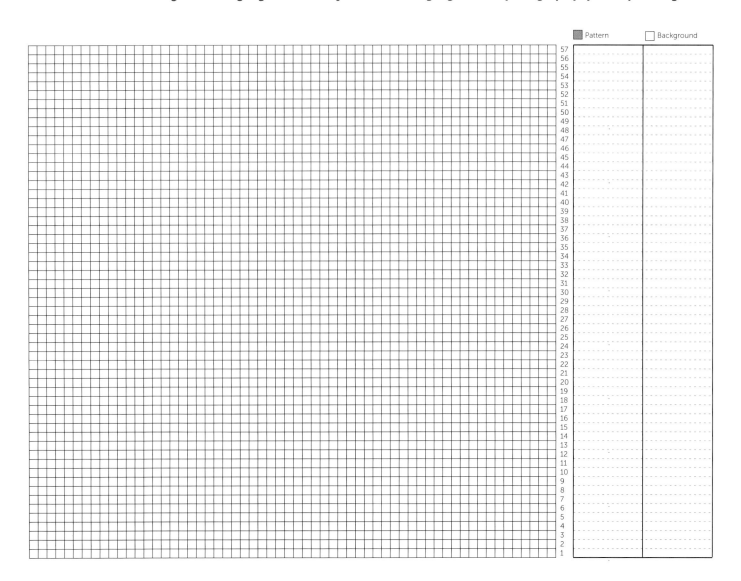

Pattern ☐ Background

Finished Size
Adult; circumference & depth depend on gauge.

Yarn
Fingering weight yarn

Needles
Body: Size 3 (3.25 mm)—16" circular and set of double-pointed needles. *Adjust needle sizes to obtain gauge.*
Ribbing: Two sizes smaller than body needle—16" circular.

Gauge
27-30 stitches and 30-34 rounds = 4" (10 cm) in pattern on larger needles.

Notions
Stitch marker; tapestry needle; coilless safety pins to mark decrease points (optional).

Stitch Guide
k = Knit.
p = Purl.
CDD = Centered double-decrease worked over 3 stitches: Slip 2 stitches together knitwise; knit the next stitch; slip the 2 slipped stitches over the just-knit stitch.
m1 = Make 1: Yarn over; on the next row, knit into the back of the yarn over.
k2tog = Knit two stitches together.

CHART & KNIT A CAP

A small cap is the perfect canvas for testing your colors and motifs. Fill in the chart—feel free to lengthen the cap if you are working with larger motifs.

Ribbing
With smaller needle, cast on 126 stitches. Place marker and join, being careful not to twist the stitches on the needle.
Work [k1, p1] until the ribbing measures 1" from cast-on edge.
Final round: With larger needle, [k9, m1] 14 times.
Stitch count: 140.

Body
Rounds 1–59: Work Chart: Cap Body, repeating the chart 7 times around the cap.

> Note: On Round 34 mark 7 decrease points in preparation for the decreases that begin on Round 35—these decrease points are shown by the single-stitch column in the center of the chart. Stitch count: 14.

Round 60: [CDD, k1] 3 times; k2tog. Stitch count: 7.

Break the yarn, leaving a 6" tail. Thread the tail onto a tapestry needle, run the needle through the live stitches, and pull the hole closed.

Darn in all ends.

Block by soaking in warm water for at least 20 minutes. Squeeze out water (but do not twist cap), lay flat on a towel, pat into shape, and let dry.

Chart: Cap Body

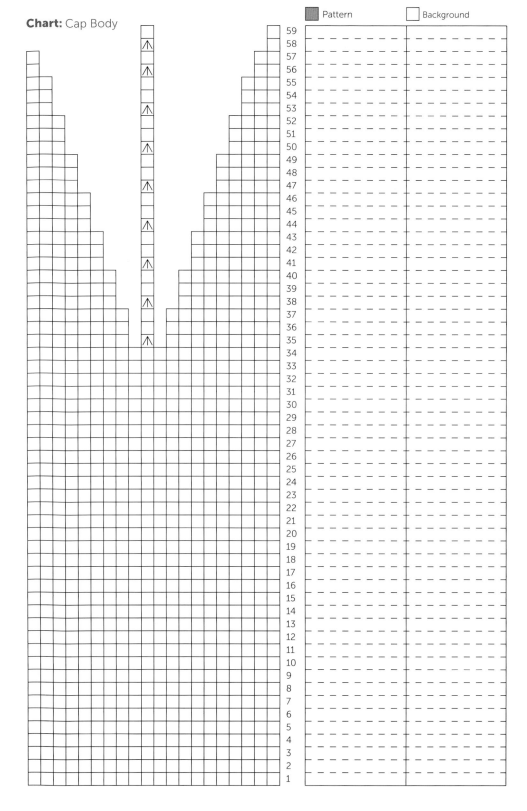

Pattern ☐ Background

59
58
57
56
55
54
53
52
51
50
49
48
47
46
45
44
43
42
41
40
39
38
37
36
35
34
33
32
31
30
29
28
27
26
25
24
23
22
21
20
19
18
17
16
15
14
13
12
11
10
9
8
7
6
5
4
3
2
1

Chart & Knit a Tam

Tams are a risk-free way to experiment with color.

Finished Size
Adult; circumference & depth depend on gauge.

Yarn
Fingering weight yarn

Needles
Body: Size 3 (3.25 mm)—16" circular and set of double-pointed needles. *Adjust needle sizes to obtain gauge.*
Ribbing: Two sizes smaller than body needle —16" circular.

Gauge
27-30 stitches and 30-34 rounds = 4" (10 cm) in pattern on larger needles.

Notions
Stitch marker; tapestry needle; coilless safety pins to mark decrease points (optional).

Stitch Guide
k = Knit.
p = Purl.
CDD = Centered double-decrease worked over 3 stitches: Slip 2 stitches together knitwise; knit the next stitch; slip the 2 slipped stitches over the just-knit stitch.
m1 = Make 1: Yarn over; on the next row, knit into the back of the yarn over.
k2tog = Knit two stitches together.

Ribbing
With the smaller needle and your chosen color, cast on 126 stitches. Place marker and join, being careful not to twist the stitches on the needle.
Round 1: Purl.
Rounds 2–14: [k1, p1] around.
Round 15: Change to larger needle. [k2, m1, k2, m1, k3, m1] 18 times, k2. Stitch count: 182

Body
Rounds 1–58: Knit Chart: Tam Body.
The top of the tam is shaped by double-decreases every other round at 7 points as follows:

> Mark the decrease points with coilless safety pins. When you are 1 stitch from the marked stitch, make a CDD. The center stitch, which is shown in the vertical line of stitches in the center of the chart, lies on top. Stitch count: 14.

Round 59: [CDD, K1] 3 times, k2tog. Stitch count: 7

Break off the yarn, leaving a 6" tail. Run the yarn through the live stitches and pull the hole closed.

Darn in all ends.

Block by soaking the tam in warm water for at least 20 minutes. Gently squeeze out excess water (but don't twist the knitting while squeezing!).

Pull the damp tam over an 11-12" plate. Rest the plate on a bowl with tam top-side up, and tug the ribbing into place. Leave on the plate until the tam is dry.

Chart: Tam Body

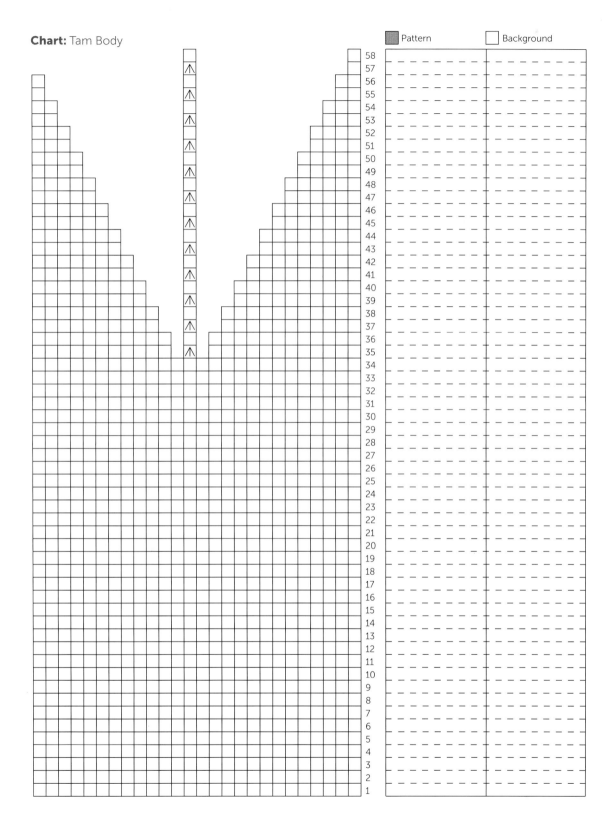

▨ Pattern ☐ Background

Chart & Knit a Pair of Fingerless Mitts

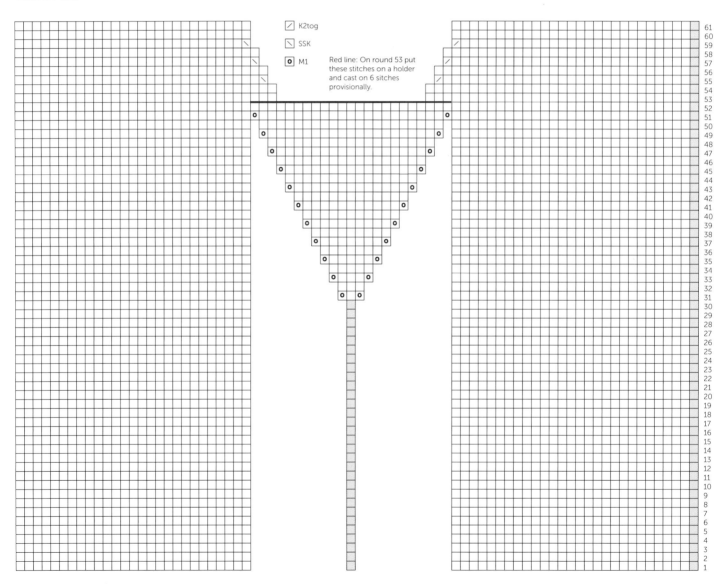

Chart: Mitts

	Symbol	Meaning
	⟋	K2tog
	⟍	SSK
	⊙	M1

Red line: On round 53 put these stitches on a holder and cast on 6 sitches provisionally.

Finished Size: Women's medium/large
(7" circumference, 8" long).

Yarn
Fingering weight yarn.

Needles
Size 1 (2.25 mm) set of double-pointed needles.
Adjust needle sizes to obtain gauge.

Notions
Markers; 24" smooth cotton yarn; tapestry needle.

Gauge
32 stitches and 34 rounds = 4" (10 cm) in stockinette.

Stitch Guide
k2tog = Knit two stitches together.
m1 = Make 1: Use your favorite—I prefer to make a loop around the needle (sometimes known as an e-wrap).
SM = Slip marker
SSK = Slip the stitch as if to knit, slip the next stitch as if to purl, knit the slipped stitches together.

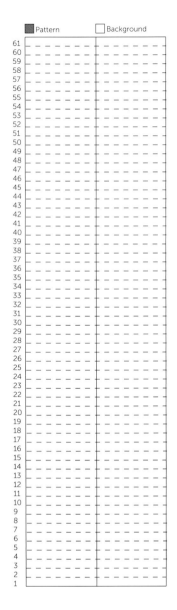

Fill in the chart with your motif and colors. Please note that the light gray stitches are "seam" stitches. Don't forget to flip the chart for the second mitt!

Cast on 56 stitches. Place marker and join, being careful not to twist knitting on the needle. [k2, p2] rib for 10 rounds.

Knit one round, placing a marker after stitch 28.

Rounds 1–61: Knit Chart: Mitts.
While knitting the chart, be alert for three required actions:

> **Round 31:** The thumb gusset shaping begins as follows:
> Knit to marker. SM. M1, k1, m1. Place another marker. Knit to end of round.

> **Round 53:** The thumb gusset ends, as follows:
> Knit to marker. Remove marker. Place the 23 thumb stitches on a smooth piece of yarn. Cast on 3 stitches provisionally, place marker, cast on 3 more stitches provisionally, remove next marker, and continue the round as indicated in the chart.

> **Rounds 55, 57, & 59:** Two stitches before the marker K2tog, SM, SSK.

Rounds 62–73: [k2, p2] rib for 12 rounds. Bind off loosely in pattern and finish the thumb.

Thumb: Using double-pointed needles, pick up live stitches being held on the piece of yarn, place marker, pick up the 6 cast-on stitches, and place another marker. Stitch count: 29.

> **Thumb Round 1:** Knit to marker. SM, SSK, k2, k2tog. SM. Knit to end of round.

> **Thumb Round 2:** Knit.

> **Thumb Round 3:** Knit to marker. SM, SSK, k2tog, SM. Knit to end of round.

> **Thumb Round 4:** Knit to marker. Remove marker. SSK. Keep the second marker in place. Knit to end of round. Stitch count: 24

> **Thumb** [k2, p2] rib for 5 rounds. Bind off loosely in pattern.

Chart & Knit a Scarf

A swatch scarf is a fun way to try out patterns and colors while creating a long, colorful scarf.

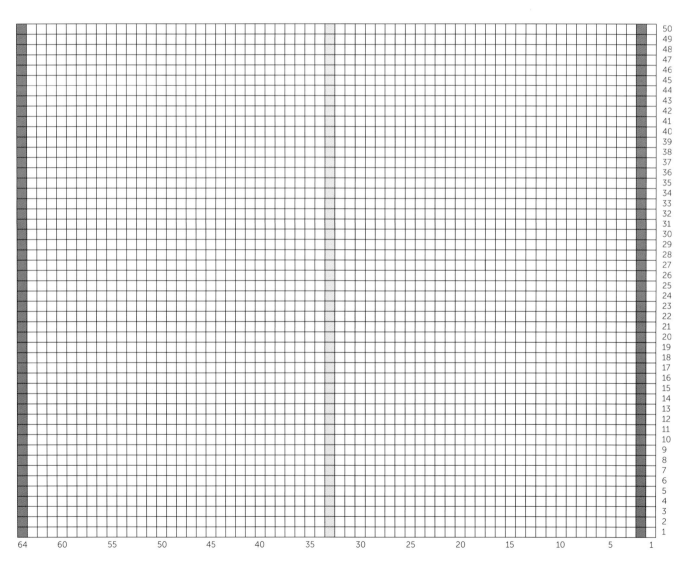

Pattern ▨   **Background** ☐

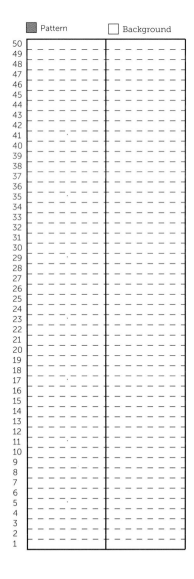

Finished Size
Width ~ 9"; length your choice.

Yarn
Fingering weight yarn

Needles
Size 3 (3.25 mm)—16" circular. *Adjust needle size to obtain the gauge you want.*

Gauge
27-30 stitches and 30-34 rounds = 4" (10 cm).

Notions:
Stitch marker; tapestry needle.

This chart represents half of the scarf—knit it twice in each round. There are 3 side "seam" stitches (k1 pattern, k1 background, k1 pattern) at each side of the scarf—you start each half of the round in the middle of the "seam."

Choose your motifs. Center them in the chart as shown on page 93 (the light gray column of stitches is the center stitch).

With a 16" circular needle and your chosen color cast on 128 stitches.

Knit your motifs and colors.

When the scarf is as long as you want, bind off, sew the ends together, and add fringe or multi-colored pompoms if you want.

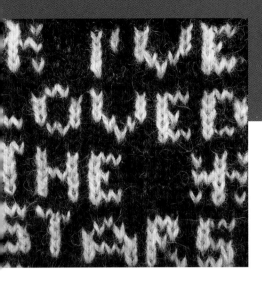

Alphabet Chart

Sign your work! Use this simple chart or make your own.

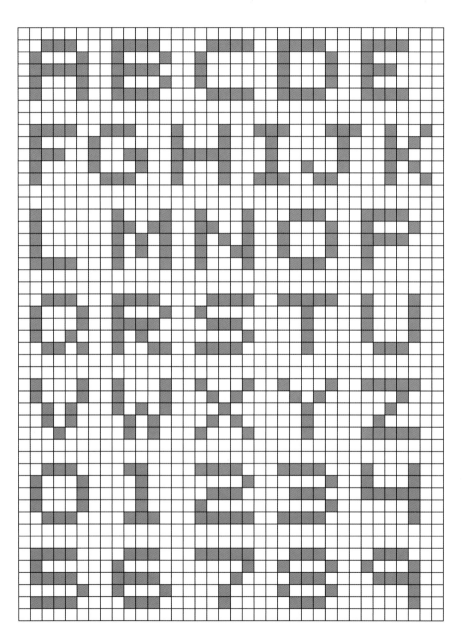

INDEX

Contributors

Lori Austin's first project as a small child was a red acrylic garter stitch scarf. She has since branched out a bit. A single mom living in Seattle, Lori mostly knits in cars, planes, trains, and ferries—anywhere she can sneak in one more row.

Renate Baur learned knitting from her grandmother in Germany when she was seven years old. She attends Meg Swansen's Knitting Camp regularly and has graduated to her first Fair Isle design. She says it was fun and satisfying.

Suzanne Bryan is a lifelong knitter with a keen interest in traditional techniques. She attended my "Design Your Own Fair Isle Workshop," where she developed the color way for her Into the Jungle cardigan/jacket. Suzanne is a TKGA-certified Master Hand Knitter; she shares knitting tips at KnittingSuzanne.com and on her YouTube channel.

Sandy de Master has been knitting and involved with wool for most of her life. She knits, spins, and weaves and operated Wee Croft Finnsheep for 20 years. Sandy currently resides in Door County, Wisconsin and teaches knitting regularly at Sievers School of Fiber Arts.

Carson Demers is a physical therapist who runs an ergonomics program for a San Francisco Bay Area medical center. Every other moment, he's knitting, spinning, designing, teaching, writing, or otherwise up to some fiber fun with a watchful eye toward ergonomics. Catch up with Carson at ergoiknit.com.

Mary Germain, former owner of a yarn shop in Milwaukee, Wisconsin, teaches knitting workshops with a focus on Latvian and Estonian techniques and travels occasionally to the Baltics. She writes about her knitting travels at marygtheknitter.blogspot.com.

Karen Hust has had a lifelong yarn jones. But when not goofing around with fiber, she can be found exploring the trails of her Puget Sound home, building twig furniture from scavenged materials, riding her motorcycle, or, more than likely, weeding the garden.

Irene Katele was seven years old when her Lithuanian mom taught her to knit, and she has not put down the needles since. In the early 1990s Alice Starmore visited the yarn shop Irene worked in, and Irene was hooked. When she isn't knitting, she's spending time with her husband, her Mom, and her three poodles in Verona, Wisconsin.

Holly Neiding learned to knit from her grandmother when she was about 5 years old. Finding Elizabeth Zimmermann and Meg Swansen in the 1990s taught her that knitting for the love of knitting could bring you joy and could serve you well in any crisis.

Ginny Olcott's best knitting design ideas come to her while she's riding her mountain bike on high desert trails. She lives in Santa Fe with her blind red heeler Cody, who is teaching her to "see" the world in a whole new way.

Karen Ritchie learned to knit as a young child; some of her earliest knitting memories are of knitting so tightly she had to force the needle through the loops. She discovered traditional cable and Fair Isle knitting books in her local library in her early thirties and hasn't looked back since.

Sarah Imber Safdar's interest in knitting colorwork started because her painting instructor suggested developing her color sense by using a medium that had static hues. Every colorwork piece she knits is a unique, personal object created for one person alone.

Nancy Sauerhoff is a self-taught knitter who has earned her TKGA Master Knitter certification. Recently retired from a career in architectural design, Nancy and her husband own and operate a small farm and orchard in Huntleigh, Missouri, where they tend to their chickens and bees as well as chase after their young grandson.

Special Thanks...

...To **Meg Swansen** for welcoming me into the world of knitting.

...To **Suzanne Pedersen**, Madrona Fiber Arts organizer, for believing in me from the start.

...To **Cat Bordhi** and the **Visionary Authors**, for generously offering encouragement and sharing information about self-publishing.

...To book designer **Kate Godfrey** (okate on Ravelry) for making this book so much better than it would have been without her. And to **Thérèse Shere** for the fabulous index and thoughtful comments.

...To the **teachers** who have shared their knowledge over the years.

...To my **students** for continually inspiring me—and special thanks to the 13 who agreed to be part of this book.

...To my many, many **friends** and **blog readers** for encouraging me tirelessly over the years this project has taken.

& FINALLY

...to **Hannah** for getting me started and **John** for being with me every step of the way. And **Mason** & **Shadow**, of course. I could not ask for a more wonderful family.

About the Author

My love affair with knitting began in 1998 when I read Meg Swansen's profile in *Knitting in America* by Melanie Falick— Meg has inspired me ever since. I love colorwork above all else, but I'm an equal opportunity knitter who usually has about 10 projects on the needles and three on the bobbins at any one time, to the despair of any minimalist who shares my living space.

Even more than knitting, though, I love teaching knitters who thought they couldn't design and make their own colorful garments. I have traveled the US teaching workshops for 10 years.

My designs have appeared in *Sweaters from Camp*, *Dreaming of Shetland*, *Color in Knitting* (an Interweave eMag), and as individual patterns on Ravelry.com. I sell Shetland yarn, color tools, and patterns for people who are similarly besotted with colorwork knitting from my online store Feral Knitter.

I live and work in a sunny Craftsman-style cottage in Berkeley, California. Oh, and my name is pronounced bay-jus.

website: feralknitter.com
ravelry id: feralknitter
instagram: janinebajus
pinterest: feral knitter
email: janine@feralknitter.com